# Student Study Guide

to Accompany

## *Exploring Your Role*
### *A Practitioner's Introduction to Early Childhood Education*

by

Mary R. Jalongo
and
Joan P. Isenberg

Prepared by
Ruth K. Steinbrunner

Merrill
an imprint of Prentice Hall
*Upper Saddle River, New Jersey   Columbus, Ohio*

© 2000 by Prentice-Hall, Inc.
Pearson Education
Upper Saddle River, New Jersey  07458

Printed in the United States of America

10 9 8 7 6 5 4 3 2 1

ISBN: 0-13-014831-8

# *Table of Contents*

# Introduction to the Student

Welcome to *Exploring Your Role: A Practitioner's Introduction to Early Childhood* and your inquiry into and discovery about your role in the early childhood profession. This Student Study Guide was written to aid your learning in four ways: (1) to help you study effectively and learn the content of the text, (2) to give you practice in taking tests and provide feedback to you on how effective your study has been, (3) to enhance and extend your understanding of the concepts of each chapter of *Exploring Your Role,* and (4) to provide an interactive framework for conceptualizing and organizing the content of each chapter. To help you achieve these purposes, this Student Study Guide has the following:

*Chapter Review*     with the Learning Outcomes, Interactive Chapter Summary, and Pause and Reflect segments. The responses with reference page numbers are in the Answer section at the end of each chapter.

*Activities*     with Key terms, Project suggestions, Application activities that coincide with the *Meet the Teachers, Ask the Expert, Featuring Families,* and *One Child, Three Perspectives* features in the chapter. Activities also include a Journal Entry page and Observation/Field Experience activities.

*Resources*     with video suggestions, additional reading, and some related web sites. The listing is not complete, but does provide another means of locating pertinent information related to the chapter.

*Quick Self Check*     has ten multiple choice questions, ten true/false questions, and two or more short answer/essay questions to test your recall and understanding of the chapter. These will also be available on the book's website for your class. In addition, each chapter provides an authentic assessment assignment that was developed to allow you to demonstrate an understanding of the chapter content through a different means – such as, an analysis paper, a philosophy of education, an article clippings file, classroom diagrams, curriculum webs and plans.

I wish you well as you begin your life-long journey of learning, caring, and teaching young children as an early childhood professional. Young children are our future and they with their families deserve our best efforts to enhance their growth and development.

*Ruth Steinbrunner*

# Chapter One

## EXPLORING YOUR ROLE AS A REFLECTIVE PRACTITIONER

*Chapter Review...*

### Chapter Learning Outcomes

- Understand the characteristics and roles of effective practitioners in the field of early childhood education.
- Consider the many different types of programs that comprise the field of early childhood education.
- Appreciate and value the contributions of early education to children, families, and society at large.
- Define reflective practice and apply the strategies of the practitioner to case material.
- Identify and use print and nonprint resources in the field of early childhood education.

### Chapter Summary

- *Teaching* is defined in a variety of ways. An important contemporary view emphasizes its _____ nature, meaning that teaching is determined by the effects of the teaching act or teaching occurs when a student learns.
- A defining characteristic of a good teacher is _____ _____.
- Based on the work of John Dewey, reflective practitioners are _____, _____, _____, _____, _____, and _____.

- How is the field of early childhood education diverse?

- Name 3-4 settings in which early care and education occur.

- In order to become the best early childhood practitioner possible, one must achieve 12 goals:

   1. Make a firm commitment to the care and education of young children.
   2. Take delight in, be curious about, and learn to understand children's _____.
   3. Maintain a positive outlook on children, families, and teaching.
   4. Understand the powerful _____ that you exert over children's lives.
   5. Concentrate on your goal of becoming the best teacher you can be.
   6. Be willing to take _____ and make the _____ that is/are part of the _____ process.
   7. _____ flexibly to change and expect ongoing challenge.
   8. Acquire a specialized body of _____ and _____.
   9. Learn to use material and human resources.
   10. Work to build a sense of _____; seek _____ and peer support.
   11. Use _____ strategies to make ethical decisions.
   12. Pursue _____.

---

**PAUSE AND REFLECT** *ABOUT EDUCARE*     Imagine that you had to trust someone else to help you care for and educate a younger brother or sister, your child, or another child you love.

1. What concerns would you have?

2. What characteristics would you look for in the person responsible for this young child's care and education?

3. When you have determined your concerns and standards, compare them with the core attributes in Figure 1.1. Also see *Featuring Families* feature questions on page 6.

- The National Association for the Education of Young Children (NAEYC) adopted a *Code of Ethical Conduct and Commitment* (1998), which provides guidelines for what is expected of early childhood practitioners.

---

**PAUSE AND REFLECT** *ABOUT FIRST TEACHERS*      *Think about your first teachers.*

1. How did they influence your ideas about your talents and capabilities?

2. How did they affect your sense of belonging to a group?

3. What were the important lessons you learned from them?

4. Did any of the teachers from your early years in school inspire you to become a teacher and play school?

5. How will you use your power as a teacher to exert a powerful, positive influence on the lives of children and families?

---

- Developmentally appropriate practice has two key components: _____ _____ and _____   _____.
- There are seven types of knowledge that educators at all levels need to acquire:
    1. content knowledge
    2. general _____ knowledge
    3. curriculum knowledge
    4. pedagogical content knowledge
    5. knowledge of _____ and their characteristics
    6. knowledge of educational _____
    7. knowledge of educational ends, _____ and _____.

- A classroom community that supports learning is:
    a. Communicative
    b. _____ - everyone expects and receives fair treatment
    c. _____ - clear expectations for and limits on behavior
    d. _____ - every person in the room is treated with love and respect
    e. _____- achievements and milestones are honored and savored

- Early childhood professionals have ethical responsibilities to (a)_____, (b) _____, and (c)_____.

- What are three reasons education is important in the early years?

  (a)

  (b)

  (c)

- Why is early childhood an important period of life?

**PAUSE AND REFLECT ABOUT** *THE BEST AGE FOR KINDERGARTEN    Read the section in the text on pages 28 through 30 and watch the video clip.  Then answer the following questions.*

1.    List at least 6 factors from the most important to least important that you would consider in determining a child's readiness for kindergarten.  Compare and discuss your list with others in your class.

2.    How do you interpret Dr. Byrd's research findings?  Do you think his conclusions are appropriate?  What other information would be useful to help you evaluate the significance of his research?

3.    What type of productive activities would be beneficial to a child whose parents decide to delay kindergarten?

# Activities . . .

**Key terms** (Match Column A with Column B)

Column A

____ 1. child advocacy (p.18)

____ 2. developmentally appropriate practice (p.19)

____ 3. inclusion (p. 24)

Column B

A.    to exert a powerful, positive influence on children's lives

B.    to help a student learn

C.    an imaginary dialogue between teacher and learners that is based on professional reading, pedagogical expertise, knowledge

___ 4. learning (p. 21)

of child development, and familiarity with a particular child or group of children

___ 5. pedagogy (p. 23)

D. to act upon one's care, concern and commitment to young children; to be a voice for the optimal development of all young children

___ 6. reflective practice(p. 7)

E. a change in behavior

F. the learning experiences are compatible for each child, including the two components of age appropriate (what children of a given age are capable of doing) and individual appropriateness (what is suitable based on the unique characteristics of a particular child)

___ 7. script (p. 7)

___ 8. teacher efficacy

G. the art and science of effective teaching

H. the continuous process of self-examination while keeping the learners' needs uppermost in mind; includes awareness of students' reaction of teacher's feelings thoughts, and of the consequences of teaching decisions

___ 9. teaching (p. 5)

I. nationwide effort to educate young children with special needs alongside their peers to the fullest extent possible

## Application activities

❖ Look at the *FEATURING FAMILIES* (p.15) feature to see a parent's checklist for evaluating early childhood programs. How do your ideas compare?

❖ Read about Michael in the *One Child Three Perspectives* (p.30) feature in this chapter and then respond to the following questions.

♦ **React** With whom do you identify most strongly in this case and why?

♦ **Research** What particular assessment challenges are represented by Michael's situation?

♦ **Reflect** What are the underlying issues?

❖ The *ASK THE EXPERT* feature provide insights from Drs. Elaine Surbeck and Lilian Katz, who respond to two questions about the development of early childhood practitioners - teacher journals and the disconnect between what is taught in preservice classes and actual experience in the classroom. Consider your own experiences with journals and then answer the following questions:

♦ What is the difference between a reflective journal and a diary?

♦      What kind of relationship do you see between the two articles?

♦      What does each expert say that is important for professional development?

♦      What does professional development mean to you?

♦      How will you continue to develop professionally?

Name_____

Date:_____ __

## *Journal Entry*

Read *Meet the Teachers* feature in this
chapter, then respond to the following:

*Compare:*     What are some commonalities that these three teachers share, even
though they are working with children of various ages?

*Contrast:*     How do these teachers think about teaching?  How would you
characterize the outlook of each one?

*Connect:*     What aspects of these teachers' experiences made the greatest
impression on you and how will you incorporate this into your teaching?

9

## Chapter 1 Observations

Visit two different early childhood programs from the list of available observation sites within the community.  Observe within each classroom for a minimum of one and a maximum of three hours and then summarize from your notes of the observation what you thought was the philosophy of the program.  Be sure to examples of activities or comments, which support your view.

a.  Name of Center:_____

Date of observation:_____  Time of Observation:_____

Age group/class observed:_____  No. of children: _____ Adults:_____

b.  Name of Center:_____

Date of observation:_____  Time of Observation:_____

Age group/class observed:_____  No. of children: _____ Adults:_____

**Authentic Assessment**    Reflect on these questions: "What do I think about teaching young children? Where do I see myself in five years?" "What characteristics should early childhood teachers possess?" "What characteristics/traits do I have as I become an early childhood professional?" "What traits/characteristics do I need to develop and why?"

Jot down some notes and ideas that you may develop further into a paper on your personal philosophy of education.

# *Resources . . .*

## Videos and other audio-visual materials...

"Career Encounters: Early Childhood Education" (28 min.) National Association for the Education of Young Children: Washington, D.C.

"Building Quality Child Care: An Overview" (20 min.) National Association for the Education of Young Children: Washington, D.C.

"The Nurturing Community" (30 min.) Video #1 from Raising America's Children video series from Delmar Press.

"Professional Ethics: a Guide for Educators" (22 min) Insight Media: New York, NY.

## Additional Reading...

Ayres, W. (1993). *To Teach.* New York: Teachers College Press.

Bredekamp, S. & Copple, C. (Eds.) (1997). *Developmentally Appropriate Practice in Early Childhood Programs--Revised Edition.* Washington, DC: National Association for the Education of Young Children (NAEYC).

Kostell, P. H. (1997). *Inclusion.* Olney, MD: Association for Childhood Education International (ACEI).

Moyer, J., Egertson, H., & Isenberg, J. (1996). *Kindergarten: A Guide for Parents.* Olney, MD: Association for Childhood Education International (ACEI).

Tertell, E. A., Klein, S. M., & Jewett, J. L. (1999). *When Teachers Reflect: Journeys toward Effective, Inclusive Practice.* Washington, DC: NAEYC.

# Quick Self Check

MULTIPLE CHOICE

___ 1. The following are all attributes of exemplary early childhood practitioners as defined by the National Board for Professional Teaching Standards **except**
   a.    adheres to a Code of Ethical Conduct.
   b.    committed to children and their learning.
   c.    knows about subjects they teach and how to present the content to young children effectively.
   d.    works in collaboration with parents and other professionals.
   e.    creates an ordered and productive learning environment.

___ 2. The script, or imaginary dialogue between teacher and learners, is based on
   a.    professional reading.
   b.    pedagogical expertise.
   c.    knowledge of child development.
   d.    familiarity with a specific child or group of children.
   e.    all of the above

___ 3. Outstanding early childhood practitioners possess all the following characteristics **except**
   a.    life-long learners.
   b.    sense of reality.
   c.    keen observers.
   d.    flexible.
   e.    energetic.

___ 4. _____ is/are an example of an early childhood program funded by the federal government for low-income parents and children that is provided in homes, centers, schools, and churches.
   a.    Head Start
   b.    Early Intervention Programs
   c.    Campus child care
   d.    Reading Recovery
   e.    Kindercare

___ 5. When evaluating an early childhood program, which of the following should be the least important consideration?
   a.    characteristics of the teacher
   b.    health and safety consideration of the physical setting
   c.    cost
   d.    age-appropriateness of materials and equipment

e.  positive guidance techniques

___ 6. Early educational experiences
    a.  define the young child's overall perceptions of educational experiences.
    b.  influence later experiences and development.
    c.  affect self-concept of the learner.
    d.  all of these
    e.  none of these

___ 7. _____ knowledge is knowing the specific instructional techniques that work best in different subject areas such as reading or science.
    a.  Educational contexts
    b.  Pedagogical content
    c.  General pedagogical
    d.  Curriculum
    e.  Content

___ 8. _____ knowledge is understanding the big picture, the overall plan for learning and how what you are teaching contributes to those goals.
    a.  Educational contexts
    b.  Pedagogical content
    c.  General pedagogical
    d.  Curriculum
    e.  Content

___ 9. An inclusive early childhood setting in which young children are educated with peers in the regular classroom, but special education services are provided is a
    a.  regular class.
    b.  resource room.
    c.  transition class.
    d.  separate, self-contained class.
    e.  residential facility.

___10. Early childhood professionals have ethical responsibilities to
    a.  children.
    b.  families.
    c.  colleagues.
    d.  communities/society.
    e.  a, b, and c

TRUE/FALSE
___ 1. Teacher reflection starts with awareness of students' reactions, of teacher's feelings and thoughts, and the consequences of teaching decisions.

___ 2. Teaching is presenting a lesson to a group of students.

___ 3. Good early childhood practitioners continually engage in a process of self-examination, all the while keeping the learners' needs uppermost in their minds.

___ 4. A teacher's journal is the same as a diary.

___ 5. Based on the work of John Dewey, reflective practitioners are active, careful, skeptical, rational, and proactive.

___ 6. The key component of developmentally appropriate practice is age appropriateness.

___ 7. The early childhood practitioner uses power to advocate for the needs of young children as well as to guide children in learning how to assert their independence in socially appropriate ways.

___ 8. Once you have developed a great lesson, you will never have to change it.

___ 9. An essential part of the early childhood practitioner's knowledge and skills will be responding to the needs of diverse groups of learners.

___ 10. William Ayers views teaching as intellectual and ethical work.


## Short Answer

a.   Describe kindergarten, nursery school, child care, family child care, primary grades, and Head Start by discussing who is served, how funded, and qualifications for teachers. Note similarities and differences in these six early childhood programs.

b.     Why is the ethical dimension so critical to becoming a successful teacher?

c.     From the chapter's list of roles in early childhood education choose the one you can see yourself involved in five years from now. Explain why.

# *Answers*

## Chapter Summary

- transactional (p. 5)
- reflective practice (p. 5)
- active, persistent, careful, skeptical, rational and proactive (p. 9)
- The field of early childhood education is diverse, because it reflects the variety of settings, populations served, roles of the practitioners involved, and the qualifications to teach. (p. 11 -12)
- See page

- 2. development; 4. influence; 6. risks, mistakes, learning; 7. Adapt; 8. knowledge, skills; 10. community, collaboration; 11. problem-solving; 12. professional growth (p.12)

- age appropriateness; individual appropriateness (p. 19)
- 2. pedagogical; 5. learners; 6. contexts; 7. purposes, values (p.22)
- b. just          c. disciplined          d. caring          e. celebratory

- a. children          b. families          c. colleagues
- Early educational experiences (a) define the young child's overall perceptions of educational experiences, (b) affect later experiences, and (c) affect self-concept of the learner. (pp. 27 - 28)
- Early childhood is a period of rapid growth, it is "prime time" for development. (p.28)

## Key Terms

1. D     2. F     3. I     4. E     5. G     6. H     7. C     8. A     9. B

## *Quick Self Check*

### Multiple Choice

1. a          2. e          3. b          4. a          5. c

6. d          7. b          8. d          9. c          10. e

### True/False

1. T     2. F     3. T     4. F     5. T     6. F     7. T     8. F     9. T     10. T

### Short answer

a.     See pages 10-11,13-14.

b.     See page 26.

c.     Answers will vary.

# Chapter Two

## EXPLORING YOUR CHILD ADVOCACY ROLE
## FROM A HISTORICAL PERSPECTIVE

---

# *Chapter Review...*

## Chapter Learning Outcomes

- Gain a historical perspective on the field of early childhood education.
- Identify the ways that teachers can function as child advocates.
- Explore traditional and contemporary roles and responsibilities of early childhood educators in providing quality programs.
- Describe the major models for programs serving young children, ages birth through 8 years.
- Articulate a philosophy of teaching that reflects an understanding of the history of the field of early childhood education.

## Chapter Summary

- Throughout history, there have been individuals who used their intelligence, influence, personal powers of persuasion, and monetary resources in the service of children and families.
  There are many different types of child advocacy activities.  List 3 here:
  1.

  2.

  3.


- The critical aspects of any child advocacy activity are:
  1. believing that ____ person can make a difference,
  2. _____ a stand and knowing to whom to turn for _____,
  3. putting the child's agenda _____.

- Child advocacy activities take many forms and use a variety of skills.

- An example of lending your voice to public discussions of positive action on behalf of children is _____.
  - When you collect and share information with parents, other teachers, and

administrators, you are _____
_____.

    ▸    Networking with other child advocates that enables you to make referrals is an example of _____.

    ▸    The Worthy Wage Campaign is one way to _____
_____.

●     The study of the history of early childhood education and an overview of the leaders enables one to gain insight into the evolution of current policies, educational innovations, enduring achievements, continuing controversies, as well as the origins of teaching methods and materials.

    ▸    _____ wrote the first known picture book, *Orbus Pictus.*
    ▸    _____wrote *How Gertrude Teaches Her Children;* believed children are naturally good.
    ▸    Father of kindergarten is _____  _____.
    ▸    _____  _____ is considered the father of progressive education.

---

**PAUSE AND REFLECT**    *ABOUT EARLY LEADERS AND PREVAILING VIEWS OF CHILDHOOD*

After reviewing Figures 2.2 and 2.3, respond to these questions:

1.    What connections do you see between the ideas of the three teachers in *Meet the Teachers* and these early leaders in early childhood education? How are teaching philosophies built?

2.    Which of these notable individuals whose commitment to the very young has made an indelible impression on your field made the greatest impression on you? Why?

3.    Did you encounter any ideas that surprised you? Any that are consistent with your beliefs?

- Many of the materials found in early childhood classrooms have a history, which mirrors the field.

  ▸ Nesting toys, child-size furniture, and lacing frames were developed by _____ _____.

  ▸ Comenius has been credited with _____ _____ for children.

  ▸ Tinkertoys, lacing cards, and modeling clay were used by _____.

  ▸ Unit blocks and large hollow blocks were developed by _____ _____ _____.

- Exploitation and abuse of young children has been in existence throughout history.

  Some of the reasons historians believe that account for children being treated with indifference or hostility in the past include:
  1.

  2.

  3.

  4.

- Four contemporary news stories are discussed in light of historical practices, which illustrate that customs, such as infanticide, abandonment and neglect, children as property, corporal punishment and harsh discipline, are the roots of current practices.

- The three historical views of children found in the present are:
  1.

  2.

  3.

- The guiding principles of early childhood programs are that young children:
  ▸ need special nurturing;
  ▸ are the future of society;
  ▸ are worthy of study;
  ▸ should have their potential optimized.

● List the sources for and influences on early childhood programs.
  ‣ pedagogy
  ‣ societal trends
  ‣ _____ theories
  ‣ knowledge of _____ _____
  ‣ curriculum standards
  ‣ community expectations
  ‣ _____ _____
  ‣ human resources
  ‣ financial and material resources

● There is a wide array of programs for the very young which vary with regard to need for, type, children served, funding, family services, goals, cultural content.

● The characteristics of excellent early childhood programs are:
  ‣ articulated or stated philosophy and goals
  ‣ appropriate structure and organization
  ‣ emphasis on concept development
  ‣ attention to all five development domains:
    – cognitive
    – _____
    – _____
    – _____
    – _____

  ‣ increased opportunity for _____ _____

- _____ for individual differences
- recognition and inclusion of the contributions of many _____ _____
- interdisciplinary approach to teaching

---

**PAUSE AND REFLECT** *ABOUT EXEMPLARY PROGRAMS*

1. After identifying the characteristics of your "dream program" in early childhood. Compare your list with the checklist in the *Featuring Families* section in Chapter 1. Reread *Ask the Expert: Amy Driscoll on Exemplary Early Childhood Programs* and *Ask the Expert: Jim Hoot on Early Childhood Programs Around the World.*

2. How have these experts enriched and enlarged your understanding of program quality?

3. What evidence do you see of historical influences on contemporary programs?

---

# *Activities. . .*

**Key Terms**   Give the terms for the definition or description given.

1. CDA or _____ _____ _____ is the national credentialing program based on course work and practical experience for entry level early childhood practitioners.

2. _____ is the ability to appreciate and respond through the arts.

3. _____ refers to social and emotional aspects of development.

4. A concept emphasized by Piaget that is the belief that children actively build their own understandings of the world rather than absorbing information and experiences is. _____.

5. _____ is the study of knowledge.

6. A(n) _____ is a person who is willing to take a stand on behalf of children and families that goes beyond common decency or expectations.

7. _____ is when children with disabilities are taught in the "least restrictive" environment in the company of their peers .

8. _____ _____ are the early childhood principles and practices that support a programs's purpose and that are directly connected to classroom practice.

9. _____ is an agreed upon set of standards for effective instructional practice.

10. _____ _____ refers to supporting children's development and learning in cognitive growth, literacy learning, affective development, psychomotor abilities, and aesthetic development.

11. _____ refers to fine and gross motor skills and coordination.


## Application Activities

❖ One Child, Three Perspectives: Read this feature in your text on page 63.

◆ *React*



◆ *Research*



◆ *Reflect*

## *Journal Entry*

Read *Meet the Teachers* feature in this
chapter, then respond to the following.


*Compare*:    What are some of the commonalities among these three teachers' philosophical
perspectives?  What are some influences that might have shaped these
teachers' ideas about early childhood education?


*Contrast:*    In what ways were the teacher's philosophies distinctive?


*Connect:*    Do you think that these ideas originated with these teachers?  In what ways were
their views alike or different from your own?  Look at the information about the
early leaders in early childhood education in Figure 2.2.  Did you encounter any
philosophies that surprised you?  Which of these notable individuals had views
most consistent with your own?

**Chapter 2 Observation**

Attend a local school board meeting.  Check the newspaper for time, day, and location.  Sometimes these meetings are telecast on a local cable channel, if so you may observe the meeting in this way.  Obtain a copy of the agenda and write a brief report answering the following questions.

1.      List advocacy groups present.

   a.      Did any advocates speak?  If so, identify the group represented.

   b.      What issue was addressed?

   c.      What was the position of the speaker?

2.      Did any teachers speak?  _____yes  _____no   If yes, what issue did they address?

   What was the position of the speaker?

3.      Did any parents speak?  _____yes  _____no   If yes, what issue did they address?

   What was the position of the speaker?

4.      What topics or issues do you feel competent to address?  Explain your answer.

## Chapter 2 Project

From an early childhood equipment and materials catalog, select 3 toys. For each give a brief report on the history or philosophy of the toy and the appropriate age range for its use. Also identify 2 toys that do not serve an educational purpose and explain why you selected them. Clip a picture of each toy to this report.

1.    Three appropriate toys
    a..    Name of toy:                                       Age range:

    b.    Name of toy:                                       Age range:

    c.    Name of toy:                                       Age range:

2.    Two inappropriate toys

    a.    Name of toy:                                       Age range:
        Reason:

    b.    Name of toy:                                       Age range:
        Reason:

## Authentic Assessment

**Problem:** On campus during evening classes young children are seen sitting in the student center or outside classrooms. Sometimes the children will sit in front of the television or will spread toys in the hallways. After talking with some of the children you discover that their parent(s) are in class and there was no child care available. What would you do?

Early childhood practitioners are often confronted with situations, which require them to advocate for young children. Using the information from this chapter and knowledge of the local community, develop a plan including the following:

1.     Identify the stakeholders.

2.     Identify potential resources.

3.     Provide the philosophical base or rationale for the solution (may be continued on additional pages).

4.     Identify the steps necessary with a timeline and who would be responsible for each step. Prepare timeline on a separate page.

# Resources . . .

## Videos and other audio-visual materials...

Films mentioned in the chapter that are available at most video rental stores:

*My Left Foot*          *The Last Emperor*
*Oliver Twist*          *Little Man Tate*
*The Dollmaker*

Videos available through your college's library or learning resource center:

*Celebrating Early Childhood Teachers* (NAEYC)
*The Nurturing Community - Raising America's Children series* (Delmar)


## Additional Reading...

Dewey, J. (1916). *Democracy and Education.* New York: Macmillan.

Hymes, J. L., Jr. (1991). *Early Childhood Education: Twenty Years in Review: A look at 1971 - 1990.* Washington, DC: National Association for the Education of Young Children (NAEYC).

Martin, L. P. (1992). *Profiles in Childhood Education 1931 - 1960.* Olney, MD: Association for Childhood Education International (ACEI).

National Association for the Education of Young Children (1997). *Accreditation Criteria and Procedures of the National Academy of Early Childhood Programs* (rev.ed.). Washington, DC: Author.

Osborne, D. K. (1991). *Early childhood education in historical perspective (3rd ed.)* Athens, GA: Daye Press.

Peabody, E. (May 1992). The origin and growth of kindergarten, *Education, 523.*

Roopnarine, J. & Johnson, J. (1987). *Approaches to Early Childhood Education.* Upper Saddle River, NJ: Merrill/Prentice Hall.

Spodek, B., Saracho, O. & Davis, M. (1991). *Foundations of Early Childhood Education.* (2nd. Ed.), Uper Saddle River, NJ: Prentice Hall.

# *Quick Self Check*

## MULTIPLE CHOICE

____1.   Individuals who use their intelligence, influence, powers of persuasion, and monetary resources in the service of children and families are called _____.
   a.   philanthropists
   b.   advocates
   c.   members of the Children's Defense Fund
   d.   humanitarians

___ 2. Of the strategies listed, which is **not** a child advocacy strategy?
   a.   Keep relationships with parents formal and professional
   b.   Speak out on issues of concern to children and families
   c.   Share knowledge and experience
   d.   Educate others about the challenges the early childhood profession faces

___ 3. Of all the early leaders of early childhood education, the first to believe that a child's education should begin before age 6 was_____.
   a.   Martin Luther
   b.   Aristotle and Plato
   c.   John Comenius
   d.   Jean-Jacques Rousseau

___ 4. _____ believed that curriculum should be child-centered and include topics of study that would enable children to understand social purposes and community life.
   a.   Horace Mann
   b.   John Locke
   c.   John Dewey
   d.   Friedrich Froebel

___ 5. During the _____ century, children were valued as laborers.
   a.   18th
   b.   19th
   c.   20th
   d.   a and b

___ 6. Although beauty pageants for preschoolers reflect the view of children as miniature adults, this notion has been illustrated in art since _____.
   a.   pre-18th century
   b.   ancient times
   c.   pre-19th century
   d.   mid-1800s

___ 7. _____ is **not** a precept of early childhood education.
   a.   Young children need special nurturing
   b.   Young children are the future of society
   c.   Young children are intrinsically motivated to learn
   d.   Young children are worthy of study

___ 8. _____ are a source for and influence on early childhood programs.
   a.   Societal trends
   b.   Educational theories and philosophies

    c.      Community expectations

    d.      all of these

___ 9. _____is one difficulty child care does **not** have.
   a.   Low salaries
   b.   Low expectations of parents and the community
   c.   High turnover rates for practitioners
   d.   Long hours

___10. _____ has/have assumed the major responsibility for preparing America's child care professionals.
   a.   Research universities
   b.   The National Child Care Resource and Referral Association
   c.   The National Association for the Education of Young Children
   d.   Two-year community colleges

## TRUE/FALSE

___1.  To be an effective advocate for young children and their families, you must believe that "just one person can make a difference."

___ 2.  Maria Montessori is known as the mother of kindergarten.

___ 3.  There are few compelling reasons for studying the historical foundations of early childhood education.

___ 4.  Enlightened views on children's early years are a relatively recent phenomena.

___ 5.  Amy Driscoll states that she avoids the idea of model programs because each program is unique.

___ 6.  Throughout history individuals, who have advocated for children's basic needs and recommended programs for them, have often been at odds with their contemporaries.

___ 7.  To achieve the best programs for children, advocates should push the boundaries of resources, of tradition, and of policies and regulations.

___ 8.  Development drives learning rather than being driven by it.

___ 9.  America has been impressed with the schools of Reggio Emilia, Italy and is imitating these exemplary programs.

_10. By working together with international colleagues, we are more likely to improve the quality of education for all the world's children.

## SHORT ANSWER

a. List three historical figures whose ideas on early education are in evidence today. Explain which of their ideas we see now.

b. Name and explain four of the sources and influences on early childhood programs. How do the influences you have chosen compare with Amy Driscoll's comments in *Ask the Expert?*

# *Answers*

## Chapter Summary

- May vary. (p.37)
- 1. a or one;    2. taking, support;    3. first (p. 37)
- speaking out on issues of concern to children and families (p. 39)

- an information source; empowering parents and families; stand up for yourself and those in your profession (p.39)
- Comenius; Rousseau; Friedrich Froebel; John Dewey (pp. 40 - 42)

- Maria Montessori; picture books; Froebel; Patty Hill Smith (p. 43)
- 1. high infant mortality rate; 2. pregnancy as an undesirable state; 3. poverty; 4. lack of ability to identify and regard early years as a valuable period of human development (p. 44)
- 1) children as miniature adult, 2) children as property, 3) children as innately bad. (pp.45 - 47)

- educational; child development; evaluation criteria (pp. 53 - 57)
- literacy learning (p. 58)
- affective development, psychomotor development, aesthetic development; respect; social interaction; ethnic groups (pp. 58 - 60)

## Key Terms

1. Child Development Associate (p.56)
2. aesthetic (p.59)
3. affective (p.59)
4. constructivism (p.50)
5. epistemology  (p.50)
6. child advocate
7. mainstreaming (p.54)
8. curricular philosophy (p.58)
9. pedagogy (p.57)
10. whole child (p.59)
11. psychomotor (p.59)

## *Quick Self Check*

**Multiple Choice**

| 1. b | 2. a | 3. b | 4. c | 5. d |
|------|------|------|------|------|
| 6. a | 7. c | 8. d | 9. b | 10. d |

**True/False**

1. T  2. F  3. F  4. F  5. T  6.T  7. T  8. F  9. F  10. T

**Short answer**

a. See pages 40 - 51.

b. See pages 50 - 60.

# Chapter Three

# EXPLORING YOUR ROLE AS A CHILD DEVELOPMENT SPECIALIST

## Chapter Review...

### Chapter Learning Outcomes

- Understand the developmental characteristics of children from birth through age eight.
- Apply knowledge of child development in early childhood settings.
- Describe the leading theories influencing early childhood education.
- Appreciate the importance of meeting young children's needs, interests, and abilities.

### Chapter Summary

- Any biological or environmental condition can contribute or impair healthy growth and development.

---

*PAUSE AND REFLECT ABOUT*    *GROWTH AND DEVELOPMENT*

1. Make a list of the biological and environmental factors that are needed to grow and develop into a healthy adult.

1. Now think about what your own development would be like if one or more of these factors had been lacking in your life. What observations can you make about the necessary resources and supports that facilitate healthy growth and development?

2. Identify some current conditions that affect children's development.

---

- All children follow a predictable pattern of development.
- The three primary attributes of what young children are like include:
  1.

  2.

  3.

---

**PAUSE AND REFLECT ABOUT**       *INVESTING IN INFANTS' BRAINS*

*After reading the feature in the text p.71-72) and watching the video clip, respond to these questions.*

*1.*   *After watching the video, list three ways early experiences affect an infants brain.*
       *a.*

       *b.*

       *c.*

*2.*   *Taking Dr. Greenspan's findings into consideration, what activity recommendations would you make to parents of an infant that would make a difference in their child's development? What would you recommend to a toddler's parents?*

*3.*   *How would you share and explain to parents the information Dr. Greenspan presents regarding brain development in light of the information in Figure 3.1 (Age-Related Characteristics of Infants, pp. 76 - 77)?*

---

- Five research-based principles of growth and development are:
  1. Development in each domain influences and is influenced by development in other domains.
  2. Development occurs in an orderly and predictable sequence.
  3. Development proceeds at _____ rates within each individual and within each developmental area.
  4. Development is greatly affected by the kinds of experiences children have.
  5. Development results from the _____ of each child's biological, physical, and cultural environments.

- Universal basic needs affect children's well-being.
  - Basic physical needs include _____, _____, _____, and _____ _____.
  - Basic social and emotional needs include a consistent and predictable _____ with an attentive, caring adult, strong _____ acceptance, and freedom from _____ and _____.
  - Minimal cognitive needs include the "ability to _____ thoughts and feelings, to _____ information in a meaningful way, to engage in constructive _____-_____, and to experience _____ both at school and in the community."
  - List five (5) other essential needs:
    1.
    2.
    3.
    4.
    5.

- Approximate age ranges that depict typical behaviors and abilities of children characterize each of the periods of development. The four periods of development covered in the text are:
  1.
  2.
  3.
  4.

- Infancy, the first 12 months of life, is a time of total dependency.
  - Physical/motor milestones include (a) increases in _____ and _____, (b) growth of brain, bones, and muscles, and (c) maturing of the _____ _____ _____.
  - _____ and secure _____ are essential for children's mental health.
  - Cognitive development in infancy progresses through sensory experiences with the infant's surroundings.
  - Learning to speak and use language begins at _____.

- Toddlerhood, the period of development from ___ to ___ years, is a time when children begin to become more competent and independent.

- The preschool-kindergarten period of development, from ages 3 to 6 years, is characterized by more complex play, curiosity, and exploration of the world outside familiar surroundings.

- ► Improved motor skills during this age lead to interest in sports, _____ games, and physical fitness.
- ► Preschoolers show increased _____ and _____.
- ► The most prominent question of four-year-olds is _____.
- ► Preschoolers like to play with language, love to talk, and are curious about words.

● School-age children, from ages 6 to 8 years, become peer conscious, social in their interactions, and work at mastering the basic skills of reading, writing, and mathematics.

---

**PAUSE AND REFLECT ABOUT**    *ATTRIBUTES OF YOUNG CHILDREN*

*Think about a child you know very well.*

1. List three important age-related characteristics that you think a teacher should know about the child to optimize the child's development. Use at least two of the developmental domains (i.e. physical/motor, social/emotional, cognitive, and language).

   1.

   2.

   3.

2. Now that you have this information, what do you think this child needs to develop optimally?

---

● In addition to child development knowledge, five attributes are essential for all early childhood practitioners in the role of child development specialist.
   1. Possess a thorough knowledge of _____ _____.
   2. Be a keen observer of children.
   3. Create a safe and caring environment for _____ children.
   4. _____ the environment to meet the needs of all children.
   5. Develop children's social and emotional _____.

- Children with special needs, which includes those with disabilities and those with special gifts and talents, are more alike than different from other children.
  - The Individuals with Disabilities Education Act (1990) lists _____ disability categories, which qualify children for special education services.
  - Children with gifts and talents need challenges to their _____ thinking and many opportunities to _____ in groups.

---

**PAUSE AND REFLECT ABOUT**      *CHILDREN WITH SPECIAL NEEDS*

*Think about a child you know or may have seen who has a special need.*

1. Describe the characteristics of the child and what you think the child's teacher did or did not do to support his or her development.

2. What concerns do you have about teaching children with exceptionalities at this stage of your professional development?

---

- The social settings and cultural contexts in which children live significantly influence their development. The _____, behaviors, _____, and _____ of individual cultures shape the children you will be teaching.

- Psychosocial (_____), cognitive developmental (_____), cultural context (Brofenbrenner), and Hierarchy of Needs (_____) are four theories, which consider different influences on development.
  - The _____ psychosocial stages are each characterized by a conflict whose resolution influences social attitudes and skills. This theory supports the value of _____.
  - Cognitive developmental theory focuses on the stages of children's _____ development. Children's thinking, reasoning, and perception differs from adults. The three stages of the early childhood years are: (a) _____, (b) _____ _____, and (c) _____ _____

▸ The four assumptions about cognitive development that underlie this theory are:

1. _____ and _____ influences interact continuously.

2. Cognitive development is initially the result of direct experience in an environment; eventually, children become capable of transforming their experiences mentally through internal reflection.

3. The pace of an individual's development is influenced by the _____ _____.

4. Cognitive development involves major _____ changes in one's thinking.

▸ The cultural context theory includes four different societal systems, each of which influences the others as well as the child's development

1. The _____ includes the home and family.

2. The _____ connects family and school.

3. The _____ might include a library or a parent's work place.

4. The _____ includes cultural influences.

▸ Maslow's theory of personality development is based upon a hierarchy of universal basic and growth needs. _____ needs form the base, followed by _____ and _____ needs.

● Multiple approaches to child development enables the practitioner to select and use whatever is best for each child at a given time.

## Activities...

**Key terms**   Complete the crossword puzzle using terms from this chapter.

*Across*

1. refers to the small muscles, such as in the fingers

8. Piaget's theory of human development that focuses on how children's intelligence and thinking abilities emerge through distinct stages

10. refers to the specific area in which a child needs individualized supports and services to help develop, learn, be happy, and be included with children of the same age; refers to children with disabilities and to children with gifts and talents.

11. refers to large muscles, such as in the arms and legs

12.	the study of changes that occur in children from conception through middle childhood.

13.	food, clothing, shelter, medical care

14.	as referred to by Maslow, include physiological needs and safety and security needs.

15.	refers to development from the center of the body outward

16.	"the ability to communicate thoughts and feelings, to process information in a meaningful way, to engage in constructive problem solving, and to experience success..." (Isenberg, 1997, p. 30)

17.	a socio-emotional disorder of known origins characterized by social unresponsiveness, poor to non-existent communication skills, and inappropriate to bizarre behavior

18.	"an inability to do something or a diminished capacity to perform in a specific way." (Hallahan & Kauffman, 1994, p. 6)

19.	consistent and predictable relationships with an attentive adult, peer acceptance, and freedom from abuse and discrimination

20.	Erikson's theory of human development as a sequence of stages in which each stage is characterized by the resolution of a conflict or crisis that influences social development and reflects the culture unique to each individual

21.	the universal sequence of developmental steps characterized by the typical behavior and abilities of children within an approximate age range

*Down*

2.	a continuum of educating all children with exceptionalities in the most natural settings within their communities, from a *full inclusion model* in which all children are educated together in the regular classroom with a team approach to teaching to a *partial inclusion model*, which provides assistance when and where it is needed, to a fully separate, restrictive environment

3.	increases in children's overall physical size, or aspect of size, such as height or weight

4.	another term for the ecological model of development by Bronfenbrenner that considers the various inter-connecting contexts within which individuals exist, such family, neighborhood, church

5.	refers to the lifelong process of adaptation to one's environment; includes growth, maturation, and learning

6.	refers to growth from the top (head) to the bottom (toes) of the body

7.	from Maslow's theory that emerge after *basic needs* are met; includes love and belonging, self-esteem, and self-actualization

8. Maslow's theory of personality development based upon a hierarchy of universal basic and growth needs

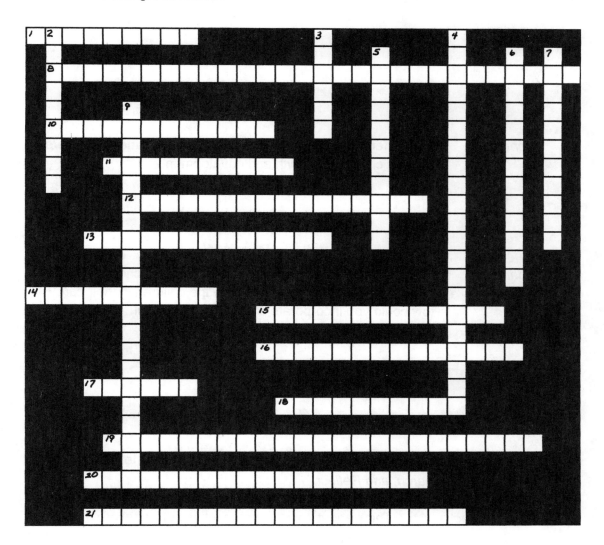

## Application Activities

❖ *Meet the Teachers* - Understanding child development guides the actions of the three teachers as they meet the needs of young children. After re-reading this feature, respond to these questions:

*Compare:*  What are some similarities in the ways these three teachers support children's growth and development?

*Contrast:*  What differences do you notice about the ways these teachers facilitate children's growth and development?

*Connect:*  What impressed you most about how these teachers meet the growth and developmental needs of the children in their care? How could you incorporate some of their ideas in your own teaching?

❖  *One Child, Three Perspectives:*  Read this feature in your text on page 103, then *React, Research, and Reflect.*

◆  *React*  Think about how the perspectives of Angelica's mother, Ms. Kane, and the social worker are alike and different. What might be some reasons? With whom do you identify most in this case? Why?

◆    *Research*    Call several adoption agencies and look on the World Wide Web to locate information and materials that will help you learn more about what adopted children are like and what they need. A good source is the Center for Adoptive Families, 10230 New Hampshire Avenue, Suite 200, Silver Spring, MD 20903 (Telephone: 301-439-2900). What key characteristics of adopted children did you find that apply to child development?

◆    *Reflect*    What assumptions about adopted children do Ms. Kane, the social worker, and Angelica's mother hold? Generate some ways you can be adoption-sensitive in your setting, such as having children make gifts for other family members on Mother's Day or Father's Day if children have only one or no parent.

## *Journal Entry*

Read *Ask the Expert* feature (p. 92).  Dr. Gargiulo responds to three familiar questions that students have about early childhood education and children with special needs. Think about your experiences with children with special needs.  Then, respond to these three questions:

1.      Would you be reluctant to work with a child with special needs?  Why or why not?

2.      In what kind of environment should children with special needs be taught?

3.      Should early childhood teachers be prepared differently from students in the field of special education?

**Chapter 3 Observation #1**

Observe two types of inclusive classrooms -- one which follows a full-inclusion model and one that is a self-contained classroom for special needs children of the same age. Your instructor will provide suggestions. The focus of the observation is on the children and the developmental levels at which they are functioning. After the observations, use your notes to respond to the following questions:

Name of Inclusive Program:_____ Age group observed:_____
Date of Observation:_____ Start time_____ End time_____

Program with self-contained classroom_____Age group observed:_____
Date of Observation:_____ Start time_____ End time_____

1.    What are the similarities and difference between the children in the two classrooms?

2.    Have children been placed in the "least restrictive" environment? Why or Why not?

3.    What behaviors were typical of children in both groups?

4.    Were you able to identify the children with special needs in the inclusive classroom? If so, in what ways were the children identifiable?

**Chapter 3 Observation # 2**

Observe two different age groups -- infants (birth to 12 months), toddlers (12 months-2 years), 2 year-olds, 3-year olds, 4-year olds, kindergarteners, first- or third-graders). Consider the behavior and skills of children at each age. Focus on one domain of development, such as physical, social, language, cognitive, aesthetic.

Program Name:_____ Age Group 1:_____Age Group 2:_____

Date of Observation:_____ Start time:_____ End time:_____

1.      How were the age groups similar?

2.      How did the age groups differ?

## Authentic Assessment

Demonstrate a beginning understanding of typical and atypical child development. Select one of the following age groups: infant, toddler, preschool, early primary, or late primary and discuss how you, as a teacher, would plan to meet the physical, social, emotional, and cognitive needs of this age group, which also includes a child with a hearing impairment and a recent refugee from the Balkans. Give a few specific examples of activities and approaches that would be appropriate for the selected age group and why.

Use the space below to jot ideas and notes for the paper you are developing. Be sure to indicate the age group you have selected and sources for activities. See the Appendix-- Compendium of Resources in your text for possible web sites and resources.

Age group/grade level_____

Common age-related characteristics:

Possible adaptations for hearing impairment:

Possible adaptations for immigrant child exposed to violence:

# *Resources . . .*

**Videos and other audio-visual materials...**

*A Secure Beginning.* Video # 2 in Raising America's Children series.

*Meeting Special Needs.* Video #6 in Raising America's Children series.

*Studying Children.* Insight Media.

**Additional Reading...**

Allen, K. E. & Marotz, L. (1998). *Developmental Profiles: Pre-Birth through Eight (3rd ed.).* Albany, NY: Delmar Press.

Black, J., Puckett, M, & Bell, M. (1992). *The Young Child: Development from Prebirth through Age Eight.* Upper Saddle River, NJ: Merrill/Prentice Hall.

Froschl, M., Colon, L., Rubin, E., & Sprung, B. (1984). *Including All of Us: An Early Childhood Curriculum About Disability.* New York: Project Inclusive: Educational Equity Concepts, Inc.

Labinowicz, E. (1980). *The Piaget Primer: Thinking, Learning, Teaching.* Menlo Park, CA: Addison-Wesley Publishing Co.

Neugebaur, R. (Ed.) (1992). *Alike and Different: Exploring Our Humanity with Young Children.* Washington, DC: NAEYC.

Wolfle, J. (1989). The gifted preschooler: Developmentally different but still 3 or 4 years old. *Young Children, 44*, 42.

# *Quick Self Check*

## MULTIPLE CHOICE

___ 1. _____ refers to increases in children's overall physical size.
   a.   Development
   b.   Growth
   c.   Maturation
   d.   Stages
   e.   Milestones

___ 2. _____ refers to the dynamic and complex changes that occur over time.
   a.   Development
   b.   Growth
   c.   Maturation
   d.   Stages
   e.   Milestones

___ 3. Three primary attributes of what young children are like include predictable patterns of development, age-related characteristics, and _____ .
   a.   cultural traits
   b.   environmental influences
   c.   essential needs
   d.   social influences

___ 4. _____ is **not** one of the essential needs of children, which influences what children will be like.
   a.   Need for guidance
   b.   Need for adequate health care
   c.   Need for success
   d.   Need for security

___ 5. An infant who is able to sit alone, uses a pincer grasp, displays some shyness, enjoys peek-a-boo, intentionally tries to make things happen, and begins to respond to requests is _____ old.
   a.   1 to 3 months
   b.   3 to 6 months
   c.   6 to 9 months
   d.   9 to 12 months

___ 6. _____ can recall and anticipate certain events they have experienced, which marks the beginning of memory.
   a.   Older infants
   b.   Toddlers
   c.   Preschoolers
   d.   School-age children

___ 7. Most _____ -year-old children can: (1) understand yesterday, today, and tomorrow; (2) identify pennies, dimes, and nickels; and (3) remember more than two ideas for a short period.
   a.   2
   b.   3
   c.   4
   d.   5

___ 8. The _____ Act is civil rights legislation that ensures that individuals with disabilities are protected from discrimination in all public facilities.
   a.   1990 ADA
   b.   1990 IDEA

c.    1986 Education of the Handicapped Act Amendments

d.    1975 Education for All Handicapped Children (EHA)

____ 9. Teachers who apply _____ theory to early childhood practice provide predictable routines, adequate health, safety and nutrition, and opportunities for children to feel like a part of a group.

a.    Jean Piaget's

b.    Urie Bronfenbrenner's

c.    Eric Erikson's

d.    Abraham Maslow's

____10. _____ model of child development includes the following four different societal systems (microsystem, mesosystem, exosystem, macrosystem), which influence the others as well as the child's development.

a.    Jean Piaget's

b.    Eric Erikson's

c.    Urie Bronfenbrenner's

d.    Abraham Maslow's

TRUE/FALSE

____1.    Growth and development depend primarily on important biological factors.

____2.    Development results from the interaction of each child's biological, physical, and cultural environments.

____3.    Experiences are cumulative, therefore they can either positively or negatively affect children's developing knowledge, skills, and abilities.

____ 4.    Periods of development refer to the universal sequence through which all children develop.

____ 5.    Older school-age children's thinking is intuitive and based on concrete, active experiences.

____ 6.    Child development knowledge is all that is needed for all early childhood practitioners.

____ 7.    Observation is a basic tool that gives you important information about children's needs, interests, and strengths.

____ 8.    The term, special needs, refers to children with disabilities only.

____ 9. Young children with disabilities are more like typically developing classmates than different.

____10. Knowing about multiple approaches to child development enables practitioners to select and use whatever is best for each child at a given time.

## Short Answer

a.     Briefly describe the changes in motor development through the four growth periods.

b.     Describe the most important elements of the three cognitive stages found in the early years according to Piaget. Include in your description the age range stage and suggestions for application by the teacher for each stage.

# *Answers*

## Chapter Summary

- 1. predictable patterns of development; 2. essential needs; 3. age-related characteristics (p.71)
- 3. different; 5. interaction (pp. 72 - 73)

-    -     clothing, food, shelter, medical care; relationship, peer acceptance, abuse, discrimination;
  - ▸ communicate, process, problem solving, success;
  - ▸ security, love, understanding and acceptance, competency, responsibility, and independence, success, guidance, respect (p.74)
- infants, toddlers, preschool, school-age
-    --    height, weight;
  - ▸ central nervous system;
  - ▸ trust, attachments;
  - ▸ birth (pp. 75 - 77)
- 1, 3 (p. 77)

- noncompetitive (p. 80); autonomy, fears (p. 81)
- child development; all; Modify; competence (pp. 87-88)
- 13 (p. 89)

- creative, interact (p. 93)
- values, languages, traditions (p. 94)
- Erikson, Piaget, Maslow (pp. 95 - 102)
  - ▸ 8, play (p. 95)
  - ▸ intellectual or cognitive
    - (a) sensorimotor, (b) preoperational thinking, (c) concrete operations
    - 1. biological, environmental; 3. social milieu; 4. qualitative (p. 98)
  - ▸ microsystem, mesosystem, exosystem, macrosystem (p. 101)
  - ▸ physiological, safety, survival (p. 102).

## Key Terms

| *Across* | | *Down* | |
|---|---|---|---|
| 1. | fine motor | 2. | inclusion |
| 8. | cognitive developmental theory | 3. | growth |
| 10. | special needs | 4. | cultural context theory |
| 11. | gross motor | 5. | development |
| 12. | child development | 6. | cephalocaudal |
| 13. | physical needs | 7. | growth needs |
| 14. | basic needs | 9. | hierarchy of needs theory |

15. proximodistal
16. cognitive needs
17. autism
18. disability
19. social and emotional needs
20. psycho-social theory
21. periods of development

## *Quick Self Check*

Multiple Choice

|     |     |     |     |     |
|-----|-----|-----|-----|-----|
| 1.  b | 2.  a | 3.  c | 4.  b | 5.  c |
| 6.  b | 7.  d | 8.  a | 9.  d | 10. c |

True/False

1. F   2. T   3. T   4. T   5. F   6. F   7. T   8. F   9. T   10. T

Short answer

a.   See summaries of each of the growth periods.  Also include general principles of development ( p. 72-73).

b.   See page 99 in your text.

## Chapter Four

## EXPLORING YOUR ROLE in FOSTERING CHILDREN'S LEARNING

# *Chapter Review...*

## Chapter Learning Outcomes

- Understand the learning processes in early childhood.
- Examine the features of authentic learning
- Explore learner-centered teaching and learning and explain the cycle of learning.
- Describe the major learning theories and their implications for the very young.
- Examine the influence of teachers' beliefs on their teaching practice.
- Consider the central role of play in children's learning.

## Chapter Summary

- Learning is the natural process of making sense of information and experiences that is fostered through interactions with others.

---

**PAUSE AND REFLECT ABOUT**      *LEARNING*

Think about one of your most successful learning experiences.

  ▸ What made it meaningful, memorable, and enjoyable?

Now think about one of your least successful learning experiences.

  ▸ What made it uninteresting, irrelevant, and discouraging?

  ▸ Make a list of the characteristics of each and compare and contrast them.

  ▸ What observations do you notice?

---

- Authentic learning develops learners who see possibilities and want to know about things. Non-authentic learners want to give _____ _____ and do exactly what the _____ wants.
- Authentic learning experiences are characterized by
  1. Using children's _____ knowledge to actively engage them in personally meaningful, purposeful activities
  2. Promote _____ thinking.
  3. Foster learning through _____ _____.
  4. Are based on each child's different _____ of _____ and displaying their _____.
  5. Enabling children to make sense of their learning by applying it to other situations.
- The role of facilitator means that the teacher engages children in learning and promotes their understanding rather than simply transmits knowledge. It is guided by the following four principles:
  1.

  2.

  3.

  4.


- A learner-centered focus addresses five principles:
  1. children's basic learning needs,
  2. _____-_____ learning research principles,
  3. _____ learning,
  4. _____ and emotional learning as well as intellectual learning, and
  5. child-initiated and child-directed learning.


- The four major principles of brain-based learning are:
  1. The brain _functions_ on different levels and in different ways simultaneously.
  2. _Feelings_ through human relationships and emotions have a profound influence on brain processes.
  3. The brain searches for meaning through _patterns_.
  4. _Learning_. The brain's tendency to seek greater complexity is enhanced and inhibited by threat.
- The four steps of the recursive learning cycle are: _____, _____, inquiry, and _____.

- Play is the catalyst for children's learning. List the 7 characteristics of play:
  1.
  2.
  3.
  4.
  5.
  6.
  7.

- _____play reflects children's ages, understanding, and games with rules.

- _____play describes children's interactions with peers and includes _____, solitary, _____, associative, and cooperative play

- Early childhood educators use multiple theoretical perspectives to understand how children learn.

- _____theory or maturation theory, suggests that growth is primarily heredity and naturally unfolding through a _____sequence.
  - Two nativist theorists are _____ and _____.
  - Rousseau was the first to identify _____ as a stage of life.
  - Teachers sometimes misuse the data from the _____ and _____approach to label children delayed.
  - _____ focuses on providing learning experience at the child's current level of ability.

- Behavioral theorists view _____ as the most influential element on learning.
  - Learning occurs in three ways:
    1. Through _____ or classical conditioning
    2. Through_____ or operant conditioning
    3. Through _____ and _____ or observational learning.
  - Name the three practices that come from behavioral theory.
    1._____
    2._____
    3._____

- Social learning theory holds that learning is the result of observation and imitation of significant models, especially parents, and that cognition is a strong influence on learning.
  - Children play an _____ role in their learning.
  - The learning environment can promote or thwart positive modeling.
  - Appropriate and inappropriate skills and behavior are learned through _____.

- _____ theory views learning as the self-regulated changes in thinking that occur from the acquisition of knowledge through which learners seek solutions to cognitive challenges.
  - Applications of cognitive developmental theory based on the work of _____ are discovery and inquiry learning and the use of concrete experiences to teach concepts.
  - Vygotsky's view of the important influence of social and cultural contexts on children's learning is the basis of _____ constructivist theory.
    - The 3 major concepts that permeate sociocultural constructivism are: (1) _____ of _____ _____, (2) _____, and the role of the adult.
    - Two applications of this theory are (1) the creation of a _____ _____ and _____ learning activities.

- Howard Gardner, a Harvard psychologist, provides a more inclusive view of intelligence, which is called _____ _____.
  - There are _____ different intelligences.
  - Applications of this theory include:
    - Curriculum approaches and assessment strategies that help students display their understandings in a variety of ways.
    - Planning needs to acknowledge different talents of children.
    - Approaches to education are _____.

55

- Understanding the diverse ways in which young children learn is a critical link to maximizing their learning potential.

# Activities . . .

**Key Terms:**   For the definitions below, determine the term defined from the scrambled letters following the definition.

Example:   _____ - an organized system of knowledge that describes, explains, and predicts behavior.   Yeorth   (Theory)

1.   _____ _____ -  Identifies all learning in terms of behaviors that can be observed, measured and recorded.    laviobehr yeorth

2.   _____-_____/ _____-_____ - learning experiences that enable children to assume some responsibility for their own learning.
dilch ditiniate/dilch trediced

3.   _____ _____ _____- situations which: 1) use children's prior knowledge to actively engage in personally meaningful, purposeful activities, 2) promote strategic thinking, 3) foster learning through social interactions, 4) are based on each child's different ways of learning and displaying their knowledge, and 5) enables children to make sense of their learning by applying it to other situations.   enthaucit  grainlen  perceinexes

4. _____ _____ - a recursive process that begins with awareness, moves to exploration, then to inquiry, and finally to utilization. grainlen clecy

5. _____ _____ - views learning as the self-regulated changes in one's thinking that occur from the acquisition of knowledge in which learners seek solutions to cognitive challenges. itviscontrustc reothy

6. _____ - any activity which is freely chosen, meaningful, active, enjoyable, and open-ended (Fromberg, 1995). paly

7. _____ _____ - also known as maturation theory, that suggests that growth is hereditary and naturally unfolds through a predetermined sequence under proper conditions. tivanicts reothy

8. _____ - one who promotes the learning by being in partnership with the learner throughout the learning process. clarfatitio

9. _____ - a support system that enables a child to move along the learning continuum by building new competencies. faldgcosfin

10. _____ _____ - approach to intelligence, developed by Howard Gardner, that suggests that knowledge is constructed through at least eight different intelligences which provide multiple ways of learning skills, concepts and strategies. ulpiltem snelgneceilti

11. _____ ___ _____ _____ (ZPD) - a concept of socio-cultural constructivist theory that is defined as the distance between what a child can do independently and what a child can do with assistance. noze fo axrimpol nelpedvoent

12. _____-_____ _____ - views learning as the individual active in shaping their own learning, and that observational learning, a cognitive influence on learning, is central to how children learn. locasi nernlaig heorty


## Application Activities

❖ *One Child, Three Perspectives* Read this feature on pages 142 - 43 in your text about Alexander's reading difficulties. Then respond to the *React, Research,* and *Respond* questions.

♦ *React:* Think about how the perspectives of Ms. Myers, the ESL teacher, and Alexander's parents are alike and different. What might be some reasons? With whom do you identify most strongly in this case, and why?

♦ *Research*    Search the ERIC Web site (see Compendium for Web address) and read several articles about second-language learning of young children. What are the key learning principles that apply to this topic?

♦ *Reflect*    What assumptions about learning to read in a second language do Ms. Myers, the ESL teacher, and Alexander's parents make? Generate some key strategies for teaching reading to second-language learners.

❖    Read the *Ask the Expert* features by Janet Taylor and Doris Fromberg and then respond to these questions.

    ♦    Which theoretical perspective is each educator referring to in their responses to the questions raised?

    ♦    Do the two articles support each other? Why or why not?

♦      Describe one or two more examples of development and learning.

♦      If your instructor provides you with a profile on each expert, in what ways do you think that each educator's background influenced her view of children and learning?

❖      Review the *Featuring Families* segment on pages 114-15. List the advantages and disadvantages to the technique described.

Advantages:

Disadvantages:

Would you use this technique? Explain your answer.

## Journal Entry

After reading the *Meet The Teachers* in this chapter on pages 109 to 110, to respond to these questions.

*Compare:*   What are some of the similarities in the ways that these three teachers help children learn?

*Contrast:*   What do these teachers think about how young children learn? What differences do you notice in the ways they have used to foster children's learning?

*Connect:*   What impressed you most about these teachers' views of learning? How do you think you will incorporate these ideas with children? Why?

## Chapter 4 Observation

Divide a sheet of paper along the long side into three columns - the first column label Behaviorism, the second Constructivism, and the third - choose either Nativistic, Multiple Intelligences, or Social Learning. Observe in an early childhood center or classroom long enough to observe at least one example of each philosophy and several examples of the one or two philosophies that are most common at the site. Note each example in the appropriate column.

Be sure to note the physical layout of the room as well as the actions and interactions of teachers and children. How does the layout of a classroom reflect the teaching/learning philosophy of the teacher. Be prepared to discuss your findings in relationship to how theories influence teaching.

### Authentic Assessment

Collect a minimum of five (5) pictures depicting children at play from a variety of sources, such as newspaper articles, parenting magazines, advertisements. Mount each picture on a separate piece of tag board with information about the picture's source on the back (i.e. name of magazine, date of issue, page found). Then analyze each picture by responding in writing to the following questions for **each** picture:

- a) Describe the situation, including what type and stage of play is depicted.
- b) What are some of things the children could be learning? Why do you think so?
- c) What could you do and say, as a teacher, to extend the play?
- d) How did your views of children, play, and learning influence how you interpreted the picture?

Clip the analysis with each picture and place in a labeled folder or section of the portfolio.

## Resources . . .

### Videos and other audio-visual materials...

*Child's Play* (30 minutes) (1978). CRM/McGraw-Hill Films.

*How Does the Mind Grow?* Insight Media

*The Importance of Play* (10 minutes), 1991. Insight Media.

*Kindergarten: A Year of Learning for Five- and Six-Year Olds* (28 minutes), 1991. Southern Early Childhood Association (SECA)

*Play and Learning* (18 minutes). National Association for the Education of Young Children, Washington (NAEYC).

*Playing and Learning - Raising America's Children* (Video 4) (approximately 30 minutes), (1991) Delmar Publishing.

*Time Together* (30 minutes), 1989. Educational Productions, Inc.

## Additional Reading...

Bergen, D. (Ed.) (1998). *Readings from Play as a Medium for Learning and Development.* Olney, MD: Association for Childhood Education International (ACEI).

Berk, L.E. (1994). Vygotsky's theory: The importance of make-believe play. *Young Children 50*, 30-39.

Isenberg, J.P & Jalongo, M.R. (1996). *Creative expression and play in the early childhood curriculum.* Upper Saddle River, NJ: Merrill/Prentice Hall.

Isenberg, J.P. & Quisenberry, N.L. (1988). *Play – A necessity for all children.* A position paper of the Association for Childhood Education International (ACEI), Olney, MD: ACEI.

Morrison, G.S. & Rusher, A.S. (1999). Playing to learn. *Dimensions of Early Childhood 27*(2), 3 - 8.

Tegano, D.W., Sawyers, J.K., & Moran, J.D.III. (1989). Problem-finding and solving in play. *Childhood Education 66*, 93.

## *Quick Self Check*

MULTIPLE CHOICE

___ 1. Recent research in _____ has contributed to a deeper understanding of how all people think and learn.
   a.    multiple intelligences
   b.    cognitive science
   c.    neuroscience
   d.    multicultural education
   e.    all of the these

___ 2. Learning
   a.    is a natural process of making sense of information and experiences.
   b.    is fostered through interaction with others.
   c.    causes a change in behavior or knowledge.
   d.    all of the above
   e.    none of     these

___ 3. Which of the following principles would **not** guide your role as facilitator?
   a.    Teachers' beliefs about learning affect children's learning.
   b.    Teachers plan a highly structured environment.
   c.    Teachers create opportunities for co-learning.
   d.    Teachers encourage social interaction.
   e.    Teachers model and teach life-long learning skills.

___ 4. Which of the following is **not** a principle of brain-based learning?
   a.    operates on different levels
   b.    influenced by feelings
   c.    requires a diet rich in water
   d.    searches for meaning through patterns
   e.    seeks complexity

___ 5. When learning becomes functional and can be represented in a variety of ways, children are in the _____ stage of the learning cycle.
   a.    awareness
   b.    exploration
   c.    inquiry
   d.    utilization
   e.    none of    these

___ 6. _____ is the type of play that emerges during the preschool years in which children make things from a preconceived plan.
   a.    Sensorimotor
   b.    Symbolic
   c.    Constructive
   d.    Games with rules
   e.    None of    these

___ 7. _____ refers to the type of social play in which children play with others in a loosely organized activity with a major interest in being with each other rather than in the play itself.
   a.    Onlooker
   b.    Solitary
   c.    Parallel
   d.    Associative
   e.    Cooperative

___ 8. _____ was the first to identify "childhood" as a stage of life.
   a.    Chomsky
   b.    Rousseau
   c.    Piaget

63

d. Watson

e. Gessell

___ 9. The application of social-learning theory in early childhood education is found by
   a. children playing an active role in their own learning.
   b. the learning environment influences the modeling of expected behaviors.
   c. modeling is the basis for learning behaviors.
   d. all of the above
   e. none of the these

___ 10. The cognitive-developmental constructivist theory of Jerome Bruner viewed learning as all of the following **except**_____.
   a. active processing of experiences
   b. dialogue and language are critical.
   c. learning occurs from the interaction of nature and nurture.
   d. cultural context impacts learning.
   e. imaginative play helps children separate thought from action.

## TRUE/FALSE

___ 1. Authentic learning develops learners who want to give correct answers and do exactly what their teachers want them to do.

___ 2. All children learn by doing hands-on and minds-on activities.

___ 3. The role of facilitator means that the teacher simply transmits knowledge to the learner.

___ 4. Play is a catalyst for children's learning.

___ 5. After seeing a production of *Peter Pan*, a project on flying begins when several children question how people can fly without an airplane. This is an example of a child-initiated learning experience.

___ 6. The zone of proximal development (ZPD) is a concept of cognitive-developmental constructivist theory that is defined as the distance between what a child can do independently and what a child can do with assistance.

___ 7. Social learning theory views learning as the individual being active in shaping their own learning, and that observational learning is central to how children learn.

___ 8. Behaviorist theory identifies all learning in terms of behaviors that can be observed, measured, and recorded.

___ 9. In socio-cultural constructivist theory, scaffolding refers to the support system that enables a child to move along the learning continuum.

_____10. Understanding the diverse ways in which children learn does not influence their learning potential.

**Short Answer**

b.      Describe the cycle of learning by identifying a skill or concept and giving examples of activities at each stage of the cycle.

c.      Respond as a teacher to a parent who is concerned that her kindergarten child does nothing but play all day in school.  How would you explain the value of play to a mother of a toddler.

d.      Name two theoretical perspectives on how children learn.  Then describe how the two are similar and how they are different as to the view of the learner and the role of the adult.

# *Answers*

## Chapter Summary

- right answers; teacher (p. 111)
- 1) prior; 2) strategic; 3) social interactions; 4) knowledge (p.111)
- 1.   Teachers' beliefs about learning affect children's learning
  2.   Teachers create opportunities fro co-learning.
  3.   Teachers encourage social interactions and shared experiences to increase learning.
  4.   Teachers model and teach life-long learning skills. (pp. 115-16)
- 2. brain-based; 3. life-long; 4. social (p.117)
- awareness; exploration; utilization (p. 118)


- symbolic; meaningful; active; pleasurable; voluntary and intrinsically motivating; rule-governed; episodic (pp.120-21)
- cognitive (p. 123)
- social; on-looker; parallel (p. 123)
- Nativist; predetermined (p. 128)
  - ▸ Gessell, Rousseau, Chomsky, Ilg, Ames (any two of these)
  - ▸ childhood
  - ▸ ages, stages
  - ▸ readiness


- environment  (p.129)
  - ▸ association; reinforcement; observation and imitation
  - ▸ behavior modification; time-out; drill and practice exercises (p. 130)
- active; modeling or observational learning (p. 131)
- Constructivist (p. 132)
  - ▸ Piaget (p. 133)
  - ▸ sociocultural (p. 134)
    - • zone of proximal development (ZPD); scaffolding (p. 134)
    - • community of learners; cooperative (pp. 135-36)
- multiple intelligences (p. 136)
  - ▸ 8
  - ▸ personalized (p. 137)

## Key Terms

1. behavioral theory (p. 129)
2. child initiated/child-directed (p. 117)
3. authentic learning experiences (p. 111)
4. learning cycle (p. 118)
5. constructivist theory (p. 132)
6. play (p. 120)
7. nativistic theory (p. 128)
8. facilitator (p. 115)
9. scaffolding (p. 134)
10. multiple intelligences (p. 136)
11. zone of proximal development (p. 134)
12. social-learning theory (p. 131)

## Quick Self Check

**Multiple Choice**

1. e        2. d        3. b        4. c        5. d
6. c        7. d        8. b        9. d        10. d

**True/False**

1. F    2. T    3. F    4. T    5. T    6. F    7. T    8. T    9. T    10. F

**Short answer**

a.    See pages 117 -119.  Examples will vary, but should correspond with what the child and adult do.

b.    See pages 120 - 127.

c.    See pages 128 - 140.  Answers will vary

# Chapter Five

## EXPLORING YOUR ROLE IN DESIGNING A SAFE, HEALTHY, AND APPROPRIATE EARLY CHILDHOOD ENVIRONMENTS

# *Chapter Review...*

### Chapter Learning Outcomes

- Appreciate the influence of the environment on children's behavior and learning.
- Use criteria to select and evaluate materials for play and learning.
- Explore the early childhood educator's role in providing safe, healthy, and appropriate settings for children's learning.
- Apply principles of design to planning and evaluating indoor and outdoor settings.
- Adapt environments to meet the needs of all children.

### Chapter Summary

- _____ is the sum total of the arrangement of physical space, the relationships between and among people, and the values and goals of the program that affect particular individuals and groups of people.

- Good environments invite children to discover, invent, create, and learn together in a community that is caring, respectful, and supportive.

- Environment has three different parts: (a) _____ _____
  (space, arrangement, and equipment), (b) _____ _____
  (social atmosphere and interactions), and (c) _____ _____
  (learning activities, routines, schedule, values, goals and daily organization).

- Good early childhood environments:
  - are organized, stimulating, and aesthetically pleasing.
  - create a caring community of learners.
  - reflect clear _____ _____.
  - protect children's _____ and _____.
  - provide appropriate materials and equipment.

- List the six *Ss* that are the unique criteria for infant/toddler environments.
    1.
    2.
    3.
    4.
    5.
    6.

- Key features of a good learning environment include ideas, people, _____, space, and _____.

> **PAUSE AND REFLECT ABOUT**     *PRINCIPLES OF ENVIRONMENTAL DESIGN*
>
> 1.  Think about a college classroom where you are now studying to become a teacher. What principles of design are evident or not evident, and how do they affect your learning?
>
> 2.  What changes could you realistically suggest to make this classroom more powerful for learning?

- Criteria for safe, healthy, and appropriate environments for all children include:
    - Arrange space to meet the needs of all learners.
    - Use time flexibly as it reveals the _____ _____.
    - Select _____ learning materials.
    - Create a positive learning _____.
    - Show students that you care about them and what they are learning.
    - Connect with children's _____.

- The seven conditions for learning - immersion, demonstration, expectation, responsibility, approximation, employment/use, response/engagement- have implications for the classroom environment.

- The five key features that reflect high-quality environments are: ambiance, privacy, density, arrangement of space, and cultural awareness.

- _____ includes light, color, texture, and noise.

- Since children have different needs for interaction, the classroom should provide a quiet, _____ place for children to collect their thoughts.

- Size refers to the number of _____ and to areas of the classroom. Small groups foster family-like feelings of sharing, connection, trust and support.

- _____ density refers to number of individuals in a space; and _____ density refers to the amount of space per individual.

- How materials, equipment, and furniture are arranged in a classroom can critically affect children's self-esteem, security, and comfort, autonomy, self-control and peer interaction.

- _____ _____ allow for self-directed activity with opportunities to work individually or with a partner, helping the child become more independent or learn to work cooperatively.

---

**PAUSE AND REFLECT ABOUT**    *CHILD - RESISTANT OR CHILD PROOF?*

Read the *PAUSE AND REFLECT* section on page 166 and watch the corresponding video clip. Then respond to these questions.

1.    List six safety and health rules that you would post in a classroom. How can you incorporate these rules into your classroom daily?

     1.
     2.
     3.
     4.
     5.
     6.

2.    What can you do to take precautions against any unnecessary accidents involving health and safety in your classroom?

3.    You've decided to have a family activity at preschool. What special health and safety precautions might be worth consideration?

▸ Cultural, family, gender, and ability differences must be considered in planning early childhood environments.

▸ The physical and visual environment should reflect the lives of the children and the families that it serves.

● Space can be arranged according to children's _____ and developmental needs, or by _____ areas.

● Planning for room arrangement should include:
  ▸ a large group area
  ▸ small group areas
  ▸ individual areas
  ▸ display areas
  ▸ storage areas
  ▸ accessible materials
  ▸ clearly marked work areas

---

**PAUSE AND REFLECT ABOUT**     *WHY THE ENVIRONMENT IS SO IMPORTANT*

Consider the floor plans shown in Figures 5.1, 5.2, and 5.3 (pp.156, 157, 158). Describe at least three features of good indoor environments that you noticed.
1.

2.

3.

Now use the evaluation criteria listed in Figure 5.9 (p. 176) to determine its quality. What message does the room convey about the teacher's values?

What changes could you suggest to make it more inviting and appropriate for young children?

---

● A_____ but _____ schedule and regular routines are foundational to appropriate indoor environments.

● Materials are the tools children use to learn. Safe and appropriate materials differ at different ages.

71

- In early care and education settings, building healthy nutrition habits is essential to children's learning.

- Planning the outdoor environment is as essential as planning the indoor environment. The outdoor environment should include:
  - a wide range of diverse activities
  - plenty of _____ - _____ space
  - easy access from the indoors
  - _____ _____ from many vantage points
  - unstructured, _____ equipment and materials
  - _____ surroundings, such as plants
  - defined _____ or _____ for different activities and ease of movement

---

**PAUSE AND REFLECT ABOUT**          *OUTDOOR ENVIRONMENTS*

1.    After reading the *Ask the Expert* with Joe Frost, what surprised you about the importance of outdoor environments? Why?

2.    How will you use this new information in your design and use of the outdoors?

---

- To make the environment responsive to all children, including those with special needs, _____ may be necessary.

  - Modifications for limited motor ability are suggested, since movement within the classroom influences participation in activities.
  - Children with visual or hearing impairments need _____ experiences to feel like a part of the classroom environment.
  - Adaptations in _____, _____, and _____ will aid children within a range of academic abilities.

# Activities

## Key Terms

1. ___ ___ ___ _E_ ___ ___ ___ ___ ___
2. ___ ___ ___ ___ ___ ___ ___ _N_ ___
3. ___ ___ _V_ ___ ___ ___ ___ ___ ___ ___
4. ___ ___ ___ _I_ ___   ___ ___   ___ ___ ___ ___ ___ ___
5. ___ ___ ___ _R_ ___ ___ ___ ___ ___   ___ ___ ___ ___ ___ ___
6. ___ _O_ ___ ___   ___ ___ ___ ___ ___ ___ ___
7. ___ _N_ ___ ___ ___ - ___ ___ ___ ___ ___
8. ___ _M_ ___ ___ ___ ___ ___
9. ___ ___ ___ ___ ___ ___ _E_ ___ ___ ___ ___ ___
10. ___ ___ ___ ___ ___ _N_ ___ ___
11. ___ ___ ___ ___ ___ _T_ ___ ___

## Clues

1. classroom materials that need to be regularly replenished or replaced, such as crayons, paper, glue, and paints
2. large, more permanent items that entail a major financial investment, such as furniture and outdoor structures
3. the planned arrangement of physical space, the relationships between and among people, and the values and goals of a particular program, center, or school system
4. According to Nel Noddings (1995) "caring for students is a fundamental of teaching and that developing people with a strong capacity to care is a major objective of responsible education" (p.678)
5. well-defined, organized areas of the classroom set aside for specific learning purposes without the teacher's constant presence and direction
6. how many people are in a given space
7. materials and activities which help children understand and appreciate their own backgrounds as well as the backgrounds of others
8. the sensory information that increases comfort, understanding and learning, specifically light, color, texture, and noise
9. how many square feet are available per child
10. regular and predictable activities that form the basis for the daily schedule and ensure effective use of time and space
11. the affective response one gets from the environment that dictates to what extent one will be a productive and engaged learner

## Project Suggestion

Research the National Playground Safety Standards and contact the National Program for Playground Safety at **www.uni.edu/playground.** Read one of Joe Frost's books or articles on playgrounds. Then develop your own checklist for evaluating the safety and appropriateness of an outdoor play space.

## Application activities

❖ *Meet the Teachers* - Read this feature at the beginning of the chapter.

*Compare:* What are some similarities in the way these three teachers design their environments?

*Contrast:* What differences do you notice in the ways these teachers encourage children's exploration and curiosity?

a. Ms. Koen

b. Ms. Endo

c. Ms. Mitsoff

*Connect:* a. What impressed you most about how these teachers set up their classrooms and arranged materials to meet the special needs of their children?

b. How could you incorporate some of these ideas in your own teaching?

❖ *One Child, Three Perspectives*:  Read this feature in your text.   Rashid's behavior, especially during Circle Time, prompts a search for a solution - a slide in the classroom!

♦ What is your reaction to Mr. Thomas' solution?

♦ What other techniques would you suggest?

♦ How would you explain the changes in the environment to parents?

❖ *Ask the Expert:.*   Dr. Vianne McLean, writing on Good Learning Environments, and Joe Frost, writing on Outdoor Play Environments respond to questions which are rarely spoken yet present in teachers' minds in their role as environmental designer.

♦ What are the most important points in each article?

♦ Relate these points to the *Meet the Teachers* and *One Child, Three Perspectives* features.

♦ In what ways are the articles similar?  How do they differ?

♦ What is each writer's view of children?

## *Journal Entry*

Re-read the *One Child, Three Perspectives* feature in this chapter and
complete the *React, Research, and Reflect questions.*

◆ *React*     Think about how the perspectives of Mr. Thomas, the principal,
             and the other kindergarten teacher are alike and different. What
             might be some of the reasons? With whom do you identify and
             why?

◆ *Research*   Interview at least two different kindergarten teachers about how
             they plan and conduct their **Circle Time**.

Teacher 1:

- How long?

- How do the children sit?

- Activities that are done:

- Teacher's response to children who "cannot sit and listen" during that
  time.

Teacher 2:

- How long?

- How do the children sit?

- Activities that are done:


- Teacher's response to children who "cannot sit and listen" during that time.



Look in <u>Developmentally Appropriate Practice in Early Childhood Programs (Revised Edition)</u> (1997), The national position statement on best practice for children ages birth through age eight, for what is considered appropriate practice for creating a caring community of learners for 3-5 year olds (pp. 123 -125) or another accessible early childhood text. Compare the responses of the teachers you interviewed with the principles in the book. Chart your findings and draw one major conclusion from your research.

Conclusion with rationale:

- *Reflect*      What assumptions about children who need to move during circle time do Mr. Thomas, the principal, parents, and other kindergarten teacher hold? Using data gathered from you interviews, generate some ways you can more appropriately respond to children like Rashid during circle time.

## Chapter 5 Observations:

a)     Observe at least an hour during the independent work/center period in an early childhood classroom. Take note of the activities and organization of the space.

Name of Program:_____ Age group:_____

Date of Observation:_____ Begin Time:_____ End time:_____

Sketch the layout of the room. Include doors, windows, and storage, as well as the names and locations of any learning centers.

1.   What activity or center was used the most? _____
   _____

   Why do you think the activity was the most used?

2.   What activity or center was used the least? _____
   _____

   Why do you think the activity was the least used?

3.   Describe the human environment of the classroom.

4.   How did spending time in the room make you feel?

5.   Write any questions about how the room was arranged and the materials used.

6.   Analyze the environment against the principles and guidelines within your text.

b)   Visit a playground.

1.   List the equipment present and sketch the playground.
     Equipment list:

| | | |
|---|---|---|
| _____ | _____ | _____ |
| _____ | _____ | _____ |
| _____ | _____ | _____ |
| _____ | _____ | _____ |
| _____ | _____ | _____ |
| _____ | _____ | _____ |
| _____ | _____ | _____ |
| _____ | _____ | _____ |

Sketch:

2.   What types of activities are available?

3. For what age level is this outdoor play space appropriate? Why do you think so?

4. Analyze the playground according to the points listed in the text and the comments of Joe Frost.

## Authentic Assessment

a. Select an age range [toddler (10), preschoolers(16), kindergarten (18), or primary grade (20)]. Using the grid provided of a classroom space with architectural elements indicated, select furnishings and arrange the space for the number of children specified for the age range chosen. Sketch the arrangement on the grid. Be sure to label areas such as storage, coats, and teacher work space. List the furniture you include in your room arrangement on the form provided and using a variety of catalogs, list the source and cost of each piece. Then justify in writing your room arrangement.

Ages of children:_____          Number of children:_____

List of centers:

Rationale for Room Arrangement:

Early Childhood Classroom for _____
(Age Range)

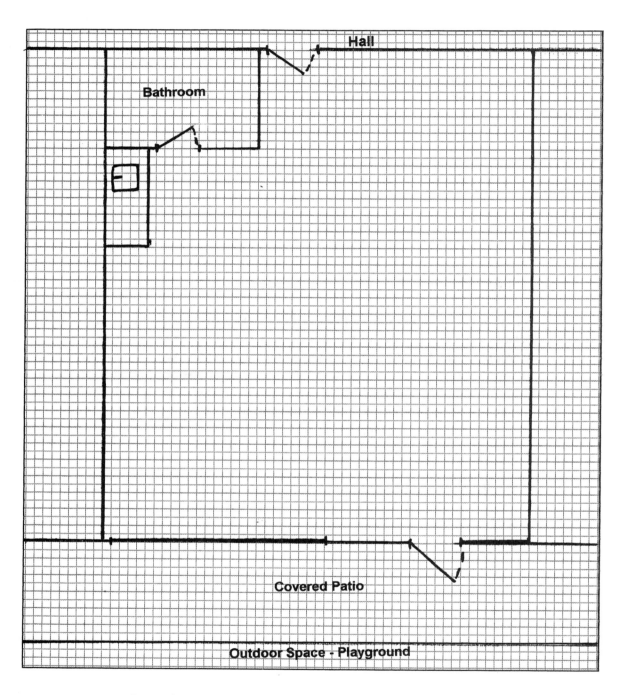

Scale: 1 foot = 2 squares

# Classroom Equipment List

| Item | Source | Cost |
|------|--------|------|
|      |        |      |
|      |        |      |
|      |        |      |
|      |        |      |
|      |        |      |
|      |        |      |
|      |        |      |
|      |        |      |
|      |        |      |
|      |        |      |
|      |        |      |
|      |        |      |
|      |        |      |
|      |        |      |
|      |        |      |
|      |        |      |
|      |        |      |
|      |        |      |
|      |        |      |
|      |        |      |
|      |        |      |
|      |        |      |
|      |        |      |
|      |        |      |
|      |        |      |
|      |        |      |
|      |        |      |
|      |        |      |
|      |        |      |
|      |        |      |
|      |        |      |
|      |        |      |
|      |        |      |
|      |        |      |
|      |        |      |
|      |        |      |
|      |        |      |
|      |        |      |
|      |        |      |
|      |        |      |
|      |        |      |
|      |        |      |
|      |        |      |

b. Select one center and list the materials you would include in the center for the month of April. Using a variety of catalogs, select the materials (books, media, games and other materials) and necessary furniture, such as chairs, cabinet, rug, and table, keeping the total cost of the center to under $350.00. List the materials and equipment with their costs and source on the form provided. Write your reasons for selecting the materials and list any materials you would make to include in the center.

| Item | Source | Cost |
|------|--------|------|
|  |  |  |
|  |  |  |
|  |  |  |
|  |  |  |
|  |  |  |
|  |  |  |
|  |  |  |
|  |  |  |
|  |  |  |
|  |  |  |
|  |  |  |
|  |  |  |
|  |  |  |
|  |  |  |
|  |  |  |
|  |  |  |
|  |  |  |
|  |  |  |
|  |  |  |
|  |  |  |
|  |  |  |

| Item | Source | Cost |
|------|--------|------|
|      |        |      |
|      |        |      |
|      |        |      |
|      |        |      |
|      |        |      |
|      |        |      |
|      |        |      |
|      |        |      |
|      |        |      |

- Teacher-made materials list:

  _____     _____
  _____     _____
  _____     _____
  _____     _____

- Rationale for materials selection:

# Resources...

## Videos and other audio-visual materials...

*Arranging the Classroom: Case Study of the High/Scope Preschool.* High Scope Press

*Child Care Video Magazine -- Space to Grow: Creating a Child Care Environment for Infants and Toddlers.* California Department of Education

*Caring for Our Children series -- Part 4: Setting Up Healthy and Safe Care.* National Association for the Education of Young Children (NAEYC)

*Concept Development in Outdoor Play.* Campus Film Productions

*Developing an Appropriate Learning Environment for Three- and Four-Year-Old Children in Group Settings.* Southern Early Childhood Association (SECA)

*High Scope: Daily Routine.* High Scope Press

*The New Room Arrangement as a Teaching Strategy.* Redleaf Press

*Places to Grow.* National Association for the Education of Young Children

*Space to Grow.* Educational Productions, Inc.


## Additional Reading...

Baker, K.R. (1984). *Let's Play Outdoors.* Washington, D.C.: National Association for the Education of Young Children.

Bronson, M. B. (1996). *The Right Stuff for Children Birth to 8: Selecting Play Materials to Support Development.* Washington, D.C.: National Association for the Education of Young Children.

Derman-Sparks, L. (1989). The Anti-Bias Curriculum. Washington, DC: National Association for the Education of Young Children.

Dodge, D.T. & Colker, L. J. (1996). *The creative curriculum* (3rd Ed.).: Washington, DC: Teaching Strategies, Inc.

Frost, J. (1992). *Play and Playscapes.* Albany, NY: Delmar.

Greenman, J. (1988). *Caring Places, Learning Spaces :Children's Environments That Work.* Redmond, WA: Exchange Press.

Houle, G. B. (1990). *Learning Centers for Young Children.* St. Paul. MN: Redleaf Press.

Miller, K. (1989). *The Outside Play and Learning Book.* Mt. Rainer, MD: Gryphon House.

Vergeront, J. (1987). <u>Places and Spaces for Preschool and Primary (Indoors)</u>; <u>Places and Spaces for Preschool and Primary (Outdoors)</u>, (1988). Washington, DC: **NAEYC**.

# *Quick Self Check*

## MULTIPLE CHOICE

___ 1. The room arrangement, space, equipment and materials are part of the _____.
   a. curricular environment.
   b. human environment.
   c. physical environment.
   d. none of these

___ 2. The experiences, routines, schedule, values, goals, and daily organization refer to the _____.
   a. curricular environment.
   b. human environment.
   c. physical environment.
   d. none of these

___ 3. The social atmosphere, emotional climate, and interactions between and among children and adults are part of the _____.
   a. curricular environment.
   b. human environment.
   c. physical environment.
   d. none of these

___ 4. The key feature of a good learning environment for young children, which reflects concrete evidence of the teacher's beliefs about teaching and learning is_____.
   a. ideas.
   b. people.
   c. resources.
   d. time.
   e. space.

___ 5. The criteria for all early childhood environments, which provide different kinds of support to each child to increase participation, achieve a sense of belonging, and become better connected with their learning is_____.
   a. connect with children's families.
   b. use time flexibly.
   c. arrange space to meet the needs of all learners.
   d. show students that you care about them and what they are learning.
   e. all of these

___ 6. Provision of uninterrupted periods of active exploration, deeper understanding, and higher-level application of subject matter is an indicator of_____.
   a.   connect with children's families.
   b.   use time flexibly.
   c.   arrange space to meet the needs of all learners.
   d.   show students that you care about them and what they are learning.
   e.   all of these

_____7. High quality environments are important because they _____.
   a.   provide appropriate materials for individuals and groups of children to work independently.
   b.   enable the adult to observe, support and meet the needs of each child.
   c.   support program goals and outcomes.
   d.   all of the these
   e.   none of these

___ 8. _____ refers to sensory information that increases comfort, understanding, and learning.
   a.   Ambiance
   b.   Size
   c.   Density
   d.   Arrangement of space
   e.   Cultural awareness

___ 9. _____responds to children's notice of differences and the environment reflects the lives of children and their families that the program serves.
   a.   Ambiance
   b.   Size
   c.   Density
   d.   Arrangement of space
   e.   Cultural awareness

___10. When adapting space for a child with limited motor abilities, the teachers should consider_____.
   a.   access to classroom and materials.
   b.   space.
   c.   computers and technology.
   d.   contacting the child's family about the child, the special need, or special equipment.
   e.   all of these

TRUE/FALSE

___ 1. The environment has little influence on children's learning, behavior, or identity.

___ 2. Although the principles of environmental design apply to all early childhood settings, differences can be found in the types and uses of age-appropriate materials as well as how different team members and families participate.

___ 3. Good environments are pleasant places to be.

___ 4. Program goals have no impact on a good early childhood environment.

___ 5. Adults' ideas about effective learning environments have changed through the years.

___ 6. The best materials for children are colorful and define precisely how they should be used and by whom.

___ 7. Infant and toddler environments have the same criteria as those for preschool and school-age children.

___ 8. When assessing your overall environment, consider the physical characteristics, the social characteristics, and the unique qualities of the local community.

___ 9. Aesthetics are not an important consideration of indoor or outdoor environments.

___10. All early childhood practitioners need to know how to adapt the learning environment to accommodate children with special needs.

## SHORT ANSWER

a. Describe how you would change a classroom or center to make it less racist and less sexist.

b. Discuss outdoor play spaces for young children and list the factors that should be considered in planning a play yard.

c. Discuss the relationship between a program's goals and the arrangement of the physical environment.

## *Answers*

### Chapter Summary

- environment (p. 149)
- (a) physical environment, (b) human environment, (c) curricular environment (p. 149)
- program goals (p. 150); health, safety (p. 151)

- simplicity, softness, seclusion, senses, stimulation, stability (p. 152)
- time, resources (p. 153)
- teacher's priorities (p.155); appropriate (p. 155); environment or climate (p. 155); families (p. 159)

- ambiance (p. 162); private (p. 162); children (p. 162); social (p. 163); spacial (p. 163) learning centers (p. 165)

- play, curriculum (p. 167)
- consistent, flexible (p. 171)

- well-organized; adult supervision; moveable; zones, areas (p. 178)
- adaptations or modifications (p. 179); multisensory (p. 179); space, time, transitions (pp. 180 - 81)

## Key Terms

1. materials (p. 152)
2. equipment (p. 152)
3. environment (p. 149)
4. ethic of caring (p. 159)
5. learning center (p.165)
6. social density (p. 163)

7. anti-bias (p. 165)
8. ambiance (p. 162)
9. spacial density (p. 163)
10. routines (p. 171)
11. climate (p. 155)

## Quick Self Check

### Multiple Choice

| 1. c | 2. a | 3. b | 4. a | 5. d |
|------|------|------|------|------|
| 6. b | 7. d | 8. a | 9. e | 10. e |

### True/False

1. F   2. T   3. T   4. F   5. T   6. F   7. F   8. T   9. F   10. T

### Short answer

a. See pages 150, 152 - 59, 164 - 65, 168 - 70.

b. See pages 177 - 179.

c. Re-read the principles of environmental design on pages 150 - 151. Think about what you would consider to be important program goals. Then respond to the question with information throughout the chapter. For example, if you have a program goal to be responsive to each child's needs, then components of an anti-bias approach would be included. Answers will vary.

**Chapter Six**

**EXPLORING YOUR ROLE AS A CURRICULUM DEVELOPER**

---

# Chapter Review...

## Chapter Learning Outcomes

- Define and describe high-quality early childhood curricula for children.
- Explore the early childhood educator's role as a designer and collaborator of curriculum.
- Identify major issues and trends in early childhood curricula.
- Understand curriculum theory and the process of curriculum evaluation.
- Define, describe, and create developmentally appropriate practices for children.
- Understand areas of the curriculum and ways to integrate subject matter.

## Chapter Summary

- Curriculum provides an overview of what children can be expected to learn and suggests ways to teach it.

- To fully understand the curriculum, a teacher needs to consider not only the curriculum standards and content, but also the intents of schooling and all of the experiences children have while they are in school.
  - The teacher's interpretation and methodology is considered the _____ curriculum.
  - The instruments used to evaluate children's progress or overall program effectiveness is called _____ curriculum.
  - The _____ curriculum refers to all the lessons that children learn about school itself as an organization and as a mirror of society's values.

- The creation and interpretation of curriculum by teachers is affected by five key influences.
  1. Teachers' perceptions about children.
  2. Teachers' interpretations of the content of material.
  3. How teachers shape the content for children to learn.
  4. Classroom _____ issues.
  5. Perspectives of the larger community.

- Developmentally appropriate practice is a way of interpreting curriculum that focuses on what children know and can do by taking into account their needs and characteristics to make thoughtful and appropriate decisions about early childhood curriculum.

  ▸ The three elements of developmentally appropriate practice are:

  1.

  2.

  3.

  ▸ Research has provided seven principles for appropriate curricula, which apply to all settings and to the adults who interact with young children.
  1. Provides for all areas of a child's _____.
  2. Supports children's home culture while developing all children's abilities to participate in the shared school culture.
  3. Sets high expectations for children.
  4. Helps children build stable, predictable, and trusting _____ _____ with adults.
  5. Is results oriented.
  6. Is worth _____, _____, and easily accessible to children.
  7. Is enacted by _____ who believe in their power to influence children's lives positively.

---

**PAUSE AND REFLECT ABOUT**     *DEVELOPMENTALLY APPROPRIATE CURRICULUM*

1. In your own words, how would you define developmentally appropriate curriculum? Include what characteristics you would look for in an early childhood setting, what kinds of activities you might see, and what kinds of activities would be of concern to you.

2. Compare your responses to the seven principles of practice just described. Tell which principles of practice your responses met and why.

- Teachers connect students to learning experiences that help them develop knowledge, skills, cultural values, and appropriate behaviors. Seven necessary areas of understanding and skill for curriculum development are:
    ▸ The primary principle of curriculum development is teaching the _____ _____ by understanding and using knowledge of children's growth and development.
    ▸ Being knowledgeable about each subject area is necessary for the curriculum to have _____.
    ▸ Understand _____ _____ or how to present content to children so they can use it.
    ▸ Help children make connections within and across the curriculum.
    ▸ Build on children's _____, _____ _____, and _____ _____.
    ▸ Realize that _____ _____ experiences will influence your role as a curriculum developer.
    ▸ Have realistic goals and expectations.

- The written curriculum contains the curriculum standards which guide teaching and learning decisions, and which includes both
    ▸ _____ standards, which state what learners should know and be able to do, and
    ▸ _____ standards, which define the degree to which the learners have mastered a particular subject matter.
    ▸ Curriculum content mean those key _____, _____, _____, and _____ that are unique to a specific academic discipline.

- There are two primary ways to organize curriculum -- by _____ domains or by _____ _____.
    ▸ The eight developmental domains are:
    1.                          5.
    2.                          6.
    3.                          7.
    4.                          8.
    ▸ Although favored by many, there are some problems with a curriculum based on subject areas, including:
    1. Expert-based, which makes much of the content difficult for children to understand.
    2. Making specialized knowledge accessible to children may lead to a _____-_____, inaccurate or _____ curriculum, which has the learner responsible for making connections.

3. Leading to fragmented skill development and the exclusion of other kinds of knowledge and skills.

- Integrated curriculum helps children connect their past experience to current learning by focusing on _____ and _____ within each subject area and _____ them to other subject areas.
  ▸ The origins of integrated curriculum can be found in the writings of _____, _____, and _____.

- The taught curriculum is *how* a teacher makes the content meaningful to a particular group of children.
  ▸ The four distinguishing characteristics of a meaningful curriculum according to Wortham are:
    1. Is relevant to children.
    2. Promotes active learning
    3. Is designed by and with _____.
    4. Links child development and content knowledge.

---

**PAUSE AND REFLECT ABOUT**     *CURRICULUM ON WHEELS*

Read the *PAUSE AND REFLECT* segment on pages 210 -11 and watch the corresponding video clip. Then answer the following questions.

1. Brainstorm a quick plan for a Discovery Van thematic unit. Choose a theme and list ideas for integrating traditional "subject" areas, such as mathematics, reading, or science. How could you integrate other areas such as dramatic play, music, art?

2. List three places in your community that provide curriculum assistance for caregivers. How could they be better utilized?

   a.

   b.

   c.

- Two primary approaches to creating meaningful curriculum are _____ _____ and _____.
  - With _____ _____ children study a particular topic using a variety of learning experiences in more than one content area.
  - Themes may be organized around _____, a topic linking several content areas, or _____ _____.
  - Effective thematic teaching should enable children to:
    1. Build on what they already know
    2. Understand basic _____ and _____ from subject areas, not focusing on isolated facts.
    3. Learn accurate facts and information.
    4. _____content and processes from all subject areas.
    5. Engage in hands-on activities as they _____.
    6. Grow in each of their developmental domains.
    7. Use the same content in more than one way and at more than one time.
    8. Capitalize on interests, because that is what _____ learning.

  - _____ are focused, in-depth studies of something that children in collaboration with teachers, _____, direct, organize, and _____.
  - Five features of projects are:
    1.
    2.
    3.
    4.
    5.

- Five theoretical orientations of curriculum are:
  1) traditional study of great ideas -- _____ _____
  2) emphasizes development of cognitive skills and thinking processes -

     _____ _____
  3) agent of change and to improve society -- _____

     _____
  4) predetermined to reach the same measurable outcomes for all students -

     _____
  5) matching students needs and interests with experienced-based learning -

     _____ _____

- Three primary issues facing early childhood educators about good curriculum according to Raines (1995) are:
  1.
  2.
  3.

# Activities . . .

**Key Terms** Complete the following word puzzle with terms from this chapter. The definitions provide clues.

1.  _ _ _ _ _ _   _ T _ _ _ _ _ _ _
2.  H _ _ _ _ _
3.  _ _ E _ _ _
4.  _ _ _ _ _ _ M _ _ _ _ _
5.  _ _ _ _ _ _ _ _ _ E _ _ _ _

6.  _ _ _ _ _ T _ _ _ _ _ _ _
7.  _ _ _ _ _ _ _ _ _ _ _ E
8.  _ _ A _ _ _ _ _
9.  _ _ _ _ _ C _ _
10. _ _ _ _ H _ _   _ _ _ _ _ _ _ _ _ _ _
11. _ _ _ _ I _ _ _ _ _
12. _ _ N _ _ _ _
13. _ _ _ _ G _ _ _ _ _

Clues:

1.  what learners should know and be able to do in certain subject areas and at specific grade levels
2.  all the lessons that children learn about school and society
3.  knowledge that is systematically organized, applies to a wide variety of circumstances, and can explain or predict a set of phenomena
4.  the degree to which learners have mastered a particular subject matter
5.  areas of children's development (i.e. cognitive, affective)
6.  studying a particular topic using a variety of learning experiences in more than one content area
7.  a way of interpreting curriculum having three elements:  1) what is presently known and understood about children, 2) planned learning experiences based on

uniqueness of each child, and 3) incorporates family needs, values, and cultural backgrounds in children's learning experiences.  Developmentally

_____

8.    _____ (second word from # 7)
9.    focused, in-depth studies that children, in collaboration with teachers, initiate, direct, organize, and develop
10.    how a teacher makes the content *meaningful* to a *particular* group of children
11.    a broad-based plan for achieving what children can be expected to learn and how to teach it
12.    key concepts, ideas, skills, and processes that are unique to specific academic disciplines, such as math or social studies
13.    interdisciplinary teaching of skills and concepts based on the study of a broad theme or concept

## Project Suggestion

Interview an early childhood practitioner about how she/he plans for the day, week, grading period, and year.  Does the teacher use a project, theme or subject-matter approach to organizing the curriculum?

Why did the teacher choose this particular way to organize the curriculum?

What features of the project, theme or subject-matter approaches does the teacher like and not like?

Teacher's Name:_____

Center/School Name:_____

Age or Grade Level Taught:_____

Date of Interview:_____

## Application Activities

❖ *Meet the Teachers* A kindergarten teacher, child care director, and a third grade teacher discuss how they develop curriculum for the children they serve. Read the *Meet the Teachers* segment on pages 185 - 86, then answer the questions below.

*Compare:* What do these teachers know about children that guides their teaching and learning decisions?

*Contrast:* How do these teachers think about the curriculum, or what happens in the classroom? What are some commonalities and differences among them?

*Connect::* What aspects of the curriculum do you think you will look for when you begin observing teachers of young children? Why do you think so?

❖ *Ask the Experts* Before reading these sections on pages 192 - 3 (Bredekamp) and page 207 (Trister-Dodge), write down what you know about and the questions you have about developmentally appropriate practice and integrated curriculum.

♦ *Developmentally appropriate practice means...*

◆     *Integrated curriculum means...*

◆     *After completing the chapter compare your responses with those of Drs. Bredekamp and Trister-Dodge.*

## *Journal Entry*

*One Child, Three Perspectives*    Read this feature in your text on pages 219 - 20 about Benjamin's school play.  Then respond to the following.

◆     *React*            Think about how the perspectives of Benjamin, Benjamin's teachers, and Benjamin's mother are alike and different.  What might be the underlying reasons?  Which perspective do you identify most strongly with and why?

◆     *Research*        Read about the appropriate roles of drama in early childhood settings.  You might want to read *Creative Drama in the Classroom* by N. McCaslin (1990); *Literacy and the Arts for the Integrated Classroom* by N. Cecil and P. Lauritzen (1994), or *Radical Reflections* by M. Fox (1993).

◆     *Reflect*          What values do all children gain from drama in the classroom? Generate a portrait of what appropriate drama for kindergarten children should look like.

**Authentic Assessment**

Additions to your portfolio for this and the next chapter will focus on curriculum. You are to demonstrate internalizing and applying the content of the chapters by developing a beginning unit plan **or** by a draft of a personal philosophy of education.

- The unit plan could be an individual or group project with products such as the following to be developed:

  (a) a chart or other visual representation prepared collaboratively, which will communicate the key concepts in the subject matter domains and salient examples. This could be a booklet with pictures illustrating the examples.

  (b) a curriculum web developed on a topic of interest

  (c) goals for the unit and skills to be learned

  (d) list of key terms or specialized vocabulary

  (e) a variety of small, medium and whole group learning experiences sequenced logically over three weeks to include (but not limited by) group meetings, class interview of subject matter, expert from community, parents, and a project. The project should include documentation techniques introduced in the class.

  (f) a listing of resources needed for the unit (i.e. books, software, films, filmstrips, videos, field trips, resource persons)

  (g) adaptations for learners with special needs.

*Or*

- Revise your philosophy of education, to demonstrate an emerging philosophy of teaching young children consistent with the principles and content of this chapter. The revision should include a description of "Developmental Characteristics of the Age Group" (infant/toddler, 3 and 4 year olds, kindergarten or primary-age), which you select, a section describing "How Children Learn", and a section on "How I Would Organize My Teaching" with rationale for selection of ideas or strategies given.

# *Resources*

## Videos and other audio-visual materials...

*An Idea Blossoms-Integrated Curriculum* - (30 min.), National Association for the Education of Young Children, Washington, D.C.

*Appropriate Curriculum for Young Children: The Role of the Teacher* (28 min.), National Association for the Education of Young Children, Washington, D.C.

## Additional Reading...

Barbour, A.C. (1999). Home literacy bags promote family involvement. *Childhood Education, 75*(2), 71 - 75.

Booth, C. (1997). The fiber project: One teacher's adventure toward emergent curriculum. *Young Children, 52*(5), 79 - 85.

Catron, C. E. & Allen, J. (1993). *Early Childhood Curriculum.* Upper Saddle River, NJ: Merrill/Prentice Hall.

Dodge, D.T. (1997). *The Creative Curriculum for Early Childhood, 3rd ed.* Washington, DC: Teaching Strategies, Inc.

Greenwald, C. & Hand, J. (1997). The project approach in inclusive preschool classrooms. *Childhood Education, 74*(5).

Gutwirth, V. (1997). A multicultural family project for primary. *Young Children, 52*(2), 72 - 78.

Katz, L. & Chard, S. (Oct 1998). *Issues in Selecting Topics for Projects.* An ERIC Digest, EDO-PS-98-8.

Kokoski, T.M. & Patton, M.M. (1997). Beyond homework: Science and mathematics backbacks. *Dimensions of Early Childhood 25*(2), 11-16.

Shores, F. E. (1992). *Explorers' Classrooms: Good Practice for Kindergarten and the Primary Grades.* Little Rock, AR: Southern Early Childhood Association.

## Web sites

Check the Appendix Compendium of Resources for possible web sites on topics covered in this chapter. Specifically ERIC from which the Digests may be downloaded and the project approach web site.

# Quick Self Check

MULTIPLE CHOICE

___ 1. The curriculum type, which refers to all of the lessons children learn about school as an organization and as a mirror of society's values, is _____.
    a.    taught curriculum
    b.    written curriculum
    c.    hidden curriculum
    d.    tested curriculum

____ 2. Developmentally appropriate practice is based on
   a.    what is presently known and understood about children.
   b.    incorporating family needs, values, and cultural backgrounds in children's learning experiences.
   c.    planned learning experiences.
   d.    all of the above
   e.    none of the above

____ 3. Developmentally appropriate practice applies to curriculums for
   a.    at-risk four year olds
   b.    special needs children
   c.    culturally and linguistically diverse children
   d.    infants and toddlers
   e.    all of the above

____ 4. The practice of children having the same teacher for more than 1 year is referred to as _____.
   a.    progressive education.
   b.    mainstreaming.
   c.    looping.
   d.    multi-age classrooms.
   e.    c and d

____ 5. The written curriculum includes
   a.    mandatory local and state curriculum standards.
   b.    voluntary standards for each subject area.
   c.    performance standards.
   d.    knowledge, skills, and dispositions toward learning that children need to develop.
   e.    all of the above

____ 6. The 20 guidelines for curriculum content for early childhood were developed by
   a.    ACEI.
   b.    NBPTS.
   c.    NAEYC.
   d.    OMEP.
   e.    none of the above

____ 7. The written curriculum may be organized by
   a.    grade level.
   b.    developmental domains.
   c.    subject matter.
   d.    b and c

e.  all of the above

___ 8.  The teaching of skills and concepts from different subject areas based on the
        study of a broad concept or theme is called
        a.  interdisciplinary teaching.
        b.  project approach.
        c.  integrated curriculum.
        d.  a and c
        e.  all of the above

___ 9.  The Project Approach is characterized by
        a.  investigation of something of interest to children.
        b.  individual and group discussions.
        c.  field trips.
        d.  representation of children's knowledge.
        e.  all of the above

___10.  Curriculum theory focuses on one major question:
        a.  How is the content taught?
        b.  What knowledge is worth knowing?
        c.  What is the best way to teach preschoolers?
        d.  What theory underlies each approach to teaching?

TRUE AND FALSE

___ 1.  A curriculum provides an overview of what children can be expected to learn and
        suggests ways to teach it.

___ 2.  A heavy reliance on words and recall enhances positive teacher-child
        communication, especially when a child's ethnic background or first language
        differs from the teacher's.

___ 3.  A curriculum based on the elements of developmentally appropriate practice
        enables early childhood practitioners to provide a realistic range of experiences,
        learning materials, and activities.

___ 4.  An early childhood curriculum centers on the "whole" child.

___ 5.  Knowledge of methodology provides a 'recipe' book for how to present key
        concepts to children so they can use it.

___ 6. All children learn best when what they are learning interests them and means something in their personal lives.

___ 7. Thematic units allow teachers to focus on isolated facts required by state standards.

___ 8. Thematic units are the same as projects.

___ 9. Curriculum expectations that are too high are frustrating to children and lead to false labeling as immature, disruptive, and unready for school.

___10. Curriculum webs are one means to visualize an integrated curriculum.


SHORT ANSWER

a.      How might cultural, socio-economic background, and home life affect what should be taught to young children?

b.      Define integrated curriculum and explain why early childhood practitioners prefer it.

# *Answers*

## Chapter Summary

- taught;            tested;            hidden (p. 187)
- management (p. 189)

- - what is presently known and understood about children (age appropriateness)
  - strengths, interests, and needs of the individual child
  - incorporates family needs, values, and cultural backgrounds in children's
    learning experiences (p. 190)
- 1.  development (p. 193); 4. relationship (p. 194); 6. knowing, meaningful (p. 193); 7.  teachers (p. 194 - 5)

- whole child (p. 195);
  - integrity (p. 196),
  - teaching methods (p. 196);
  - interests, cultural backgrounds;
  - prior knowledge; personal life (p. 196)
- content,
  - performance (p. 196)
  - concepts, ideas, skills, processes (p. 198)
- developmental, subject matter (p. 199)
  - cognitive, social, affective, aesthetic, physical, imaginative, language, construction (p. 205)
  - 2. watered-down, confusing (p. 205)

- processes, concepts, connecting (p. 206)
  - Dewey, Piaget, Kilpatrick (p.  206)
- 3. children (p.  208)

- thematic units, projects (p. 211)
  - thematic units (p. 211)
  - literature, multiple intelligences (p. 211)
  - 2.  concepts, processes; 4. integrate; 5. inquire; 8. motivates (p. 213)
  - projects; initiate, develop (p. 214)
  - (1) individual and group discussions, (2) field trips, (3) representation of children's knowledge, (4) investigations, (5) displays of learning (p. 214)
- 1) academic rationalist, 2) cognitive processes, 3) social reconstruction, 4) technology, 5) personal relevance (p. 219)

- 1) time to present the curriculum, 2) the academic nature of curriculum for young children, and 3) depth versus breadth decisions.  (p. 219)

**Key Terms**

1. content standards (p.198)
2. hidden curriculum (p.187)
3. theory (p.217)
4. performance standards (p.198)
5. developmental domains (p.204)
6. theme teaching (p. 211)

7-8. developmentally appropriate practice (pp. 189-90)
9. projects (p.214)
10. taught curriculum (p.206)
11. curriculum (p.187)
12. curriculum content: (p.198)
13. integrated curriculum (pp.205-6)

*Quick Self Check*

Multiple Choice

| | | | | |
|---|---|---|---|---|
| 1. c | 2. d | 3. e | 4. e | 5. e |
| 6. c | 7. d | 8. d | 9. e | 10. b |

True/False

1. T   2. F   3. T   4. T   5. F   6. T   7. F   8. F   9. T   10. T

Short answer

a. See page196 about your role as a curriculum developer and the areas of knowledge and expertise required. Numbers 3, 4, and 5 relate directly to this question, as does a thorough understanding of developmentally appropriate practice.

b. Pages 206 through 209 address the characteristics of the taught curriculum and how to make curriculum meaningful to children. It is preferred because it promotes active learning by the children, is designed by and with children, and is relevant to what children are interested in and need to know. Most of all it makes the link between child development and content knowledge, so the whole child may be taught and all developmental domains may progress.

# Chapter Seven

# EXPLORING YOUR ROLE IN PLANNING FOR CHILDREN'S LEARNING

## Chapter Review...

### Chapter Learning Outcomes

- Define and describe types and levels of planning.
- Investigate the purpose of planning and its role in effective instruction.
- Apply principles of planning to lessons, thematic units, and projects.
- Develop daily, weekly, and monthly schedules to meet goals and objectives.
- Plan for individual needs and abilities of diverse learners.

### Chapter Summary

- Planning for teaching involves creating and arranging events in your mind that helps you manage time and events and make decisions that will benefit each child.  Teachers include planning for:
  - a supportive _____,
  - routines and procedures,
  - _____ between activities,
  - children's _____ and needs.

- Teachers engage in two basic types of planning: long-term and short-term.
  - Long-term planning involves decisions about _____ and _____ to cover, the _____ in which topics are covered, and the amount of _____ to spend on each topic.
  - Long term plans need to be _____ to meet the changing needs, interests, and abilities of the children.
  - Short-term planning addresses the day-to-day decisions and includes _____ and _____ plans.
  - Good planning provides self-selected learning activities with carefully prepared _____.

## TAKE A SECOND LOOK AT  PLANS

Carefully review Figures 7.1 through 7.6 on pages 230 - 244.  Long-term and short-term planning examples for different age levels are provided.  Select one area of development, such as physical, social, or language, and note how the planning is similar and different across ages.  Consider types of activities and topics.

1.    What did you expect to find?  Why?

2.    What surprised you about the plans?  Why?

3.    How was flexibility built into the plans?

- As a planner, the practitioner's responsibility is for:
    - what happens when children are in the classroom,
    - for selecting and establishing appropriate _____ and _____,
    - for _____ ____ _____ for learning, and
    - for _____ and _____ children's progress.

- The essential components of good planning are:
    1.    Know the children for whom you are planning.
    2.    Be knowledgeable about the content and concepts you plan to teach.
    3.    Plan a variety of experiences to meet individual needs, abilities, and interests.
    4.    Plan appropriate methods for assessing and evaluating children's learning.  KWL strategy assess children's prior knowledge by asking (1) What do I K_____? (2) What do I W_____to know? (3) What I have L_____.
    5.    Plan time to _____ upon your teaching and learning activities.
    6.    Allow plenty of time to plan ahead.

110

1.    Think about your role as a planner in relation to the unit on families described on pages 236 - 244.  What did you realize about planning when you read about these student teachers' plans?

2.    What questions do you have from reading this description?

3.    With what do you agree and disagree?

4.    What other thoughts do you have about planning a unit on families for kindergarten children?

● Planning is an essential aspect of successful teaching.
  ▸ Grouping facilitates individual learning.  The four types of grouping patterns are:
    1.
    2.
    3.
    4.
  ▸ As a teacher, having clear goals for students facilitates planning accountability to local, state and national standards.
  ▸ As a teacher who wants to improve your teaching and enable children's learning, an important goal is to _____ _____.

  ▸ List six of the functions of good planning.
    1.

    2.

    3.

    4.

    5.

    6.

1.      Re-read the opening section, *Meet the Teachers (pp. 225 - 26)*.  How might these
        teachers have planned differently?


2.      What would be the advantages and disadvantages of alternative approaches?


- Research describes the qualitative differences in the planning process between
  preservice and experienced teachers.  Write two differences between a novice
  and an experienced teacher.
  a.

  b.


- Four basic elements of long- and short-term planning are: (1) goals and
  objectives, (2) processes, (3) activities and lessons, and (4) _____.


- _____ is a way to brainstorm key concepts, ideas, and learning
  experiences.


- The two kinds of long-range plans are (a) planning for _____ _____
  and planning for _____.


- A _____ concept is a broad idea, question or problem that helps children
  make connections and further their understanding of the world and is the focus of
  a thematic unit.


- The three steps of planning projects are:
  1.
  2.
  3.

1.      Re-read both *Ask the Expert* features (pp. 258 - 59 and 262 - 63). Search the Internet for suggestions for projects and units. What did you find that would be useful to your planning?

2.      What criteria will you use for judging the worthiness of units and projects located on the Internet?

3.      What questions do you still have?

- Activity and lesson plans take many forms, but they should be complete enough so that any teacher can pick one up and know for any given day what is planned and why it is planned.

- To achieve the best outcomes for children's learning and development, practitioners must become knowledgeable about and skilled in the various techniques of planning.

# *Activities...*

**Key terms** (Match Column A with Column B

Column A

_____ 1. accountability (p. 249)

_____ 2. long-term planning(p. 227)

_____ 3. planning   (p.227)

Column B

A.      broad purposes for learning
B.      refers to a single teaching episode
C.      refers to teaching students to conform to the demands of the written material through group instruction of small, digestible pieces of information.

_____ 4. projects (p.259)

_____ 5. webbing (p. 255)

_____ 6. activity or lesson (p. 261)

_____ 7. thematic unit (p. 259)

_____ 8. cognitive monitoring strategies (pp. 248 - 49)

_____ 9. objectives (p. 255)

_____ 10. direct instruction model

_____ 11. goals (p. 255)

_____ 12. short-term planning (p. 228)

D.  means reporting regular evaluation of progress by students, staff, teachers, and of the program for future planning

E.  refers to the visualizing, guiding, managing, decision- making and self-probing teachers use in planning

F.  defines the specific skills, behavior, or concept the learner is to acquire

G.  very general and includes yearly planning, semester or quarterly planning, and unit or project planning

H.  specific and detailed plans, which identify activities, experiences, and lessons to be used in the classroom on a day-to-day basis

I.  pictorial or graphic representation that connects possible key concepts, ideas, and learning experiences in planning

J.  the ability to think ahead and anticipate; in education, refers to the thinking and rethinking about teaching and learning

K.  planned, in-depth investigations of a topic worth learning about, with the goal of learning more by applying higher-level thinking skills

L.  one manageable way of providing a variety of learning experiences around a core concept; method of study and focus change with the age, interests and grade level of the children

## Project Suggestion

Talk with three early childhood practitioners to discuss how they develop daily lesson plans. Do they plan individually or in a group? What are the advantages and disadvantages these teachers see in individual and cooperative planning? Which do you prefer and explain why?

## Application Activities

❖   _Featuring Families_

♦   One way to share themes with families is to send home a monthly calendar with activities related to the particular themes under study to extend and reinforce learning. What themes, concepts, or skills are found on this home activity calendar?

♦       Since only three weeks of February are given, complete a final week of home activities on the calendar below..

| February Home Activities | | | | |
|---|---|---|---|---|
| **Monday** | **Tuesday** | **Wednesday** | **Thursday** | **Friday** |
| 23 | 24 | 25 | 26 | 27 |

❖     *One Child, Three Perspectives*     Re-read this feature on pages 270 - 71. The expectations and perspectives of Shayna, her teacher, and her parents for kindergarten are very different.

♦      ***React***    Think about how the perspectives of Shayna, her parents, and Shayna's teacher are alike and different. What might be some reasons? With whom do you most closely identify and why?

♦      ***Research***     Shayna's teacher is using the direct instruction model of teaching. Compare this way of teaching with thematic units and projects, as described by Marjorie Kostelnik and Jeanette Allison in the *Ask the Expert* features of this chapter.

Consider again the kindergarten unit on families developed by the five student teachers. How did they plan to promote concepts and skills while using theme teaching?

♦  **Reflect**    What alternatives does Shayna's teacher have in planning to meet Shayna's needs and keep her interested in kindergarten?

❖  *In Class Workshop*    Using the *Developmental Milestones* for children described in Tables 3.1 through 3.4 in Chapter 3, examine the Learning Plan below and consider each of the three categories. Next, think about a child you know very well. It may be your own child, a niece, nephew, or someone from your field experience class. Fill out the Learning Plan for that child.

```
┌─────────────────────────────────────────────────────────────────┐
│                          Learning Plan                          │
│                                                                 │
│  Name    _____             │
│  Date    _____             │
│                                                                 │
│  Areas of Strength and Confidence                               │
│  1.      _____             │
│  2.      _____             │
│  3.      _____             │
│                                                                 │
│  Areas Needing Strengthening                                    │
│   1.     _____             │
│   2.     _____             │
│   3.     _____             │
│                                                                 │
│  Activities to Help                                             │
│  1.      _____             │
│  2.      _____             │
│  3.      _____             │
│                                                                 │
└─────────────────────────────────────────────────────────────────┘
```

♦ What information do you have that does not fit on the chart?

♦ Compile your individual learning plan information with other students into a classroom chart that allows for easy access to implementation.

♦ How do you think Learning Plans can improve children's learning?

## Journal Entry

Re-read the *Meet the Teachers* segment, then respond to these questions.

*Compare:*   What are some similarities in the way these teacher's plan for children's learning?

*Contrast:*   What differences do you notice in how these teachers plan?

*Connect:*   What surprised you about how these teachers plan for all children? What ideas do you think will be most useful for your planning? Why?

**Chapter 7 Observations:** Observe a free play period in a toddler or preschool classroom. Using the following form label headings for each content area you see represented in some way. Write down the activity and the children's interactions that suggest a preparation for more formal curricular study later.

Name of Center_____ Age group observed_____

Observation date_____ Begin time_____ End time_____

Number of children _____

| Content Area | | | | |
|---|---|---|---|---|
| Activity | | | | |
| Children's Interactions | | | | |
| Activity | | | | |
| Children's Interaction | | | | |

## Authentic Assessment

The thematic unit introduced in Chapter 6 is continued. Use the lesson plan form at the end of this guide and add detailed lesson plans for one week of the thematic unit. Also, prepare a classroom learning plan chart (see form at end of guide) for the age group of your unit, based on the child descriptions compiled during the In-Class Workshop.

# *Resources...*

## Videos and other audio-visual materials...

*Appropriate Curriculum for Young Children: The Role of the Teacher* (28 minutes). National Association for the Education of Young Children (NAEYC).

*Goal Setting for Early Childhood : A Partnership in Action* (1991, 21 minutes). Creative Educational Video.

*Small Group Time Video Series.* (1988). High/Scope.

*Supporting Children's Active Learning.* (1989, 13 minutes). High/Scope.

## Additional Reading...

Curtis, D. & Carter, M. (1997). *Reflecting Children's Lives: A Handbook for Planning Child-centered Curriculum.* Seattle, WA: Harvest Resources.

Jones, E. (1994). *Emergent Curriculum.* Washington, DC: National Association for the Education of Young Children.

Katz, L. & Chard, S. (Oct 1998). *Issues in Selecting Topics for Projects.* An ERIC Digest, EDO-PS-98-8.

Shores, F. E. (1992). *Explorers' Classrooms: Good Practice for Kindergarten and the Primary Grades.* Little Rock, AR: Southern Early Childhood Association.

# Quick Self Check

## MULTIPLE CHOICE

___ 1. Which of the following is **not** a characteristic of long-term planning?
    a.      based on detailed knowledge of children's prior experience
    b.      provides direction for a program
    c.      contains broad goals, objectives, concepts and skills
    d.      is flexible

___ 2. Short-term planning
    a.      addresses day-to-day decisions.
    b.      includes daily and weekly plans that identify activities and experiences.
    c.      contain specific objectives.
    d.      relates to children's needs and supports their development.
    e.      all of the above

___ 3. When planning is flexible, a practitioner can
    a.      capitalize on unanticipated learning opportunities.
    b.      develop reasonable goals for each child.
    c.      include families in the plans.
    d.      a and b
    e.      all of the above

___ 4. Teachers plan to make decisions about
    a.      individual and group learning.
    b.      accountability to local, state, and national standards.
    c.      each learner's success.
    d.      b and c
    e.      all of the above

___ 5. Grouping should
    a.      vary in size consistent with the activity.
    b.      foster self-esteem and social learning.
    c.      allow for teacher-initiated activities.
    d.      be paced appropriately to enhance learning.
    e.      a, b, and d

___ 6. Some important strategies for meeting the needs of culturally and ethnically diverse learners are
    a.      use audio-taped materials.
    b.      incorporate thematic units and projects.
    c.      emphasize one-on-one interactions.

d. all of these

e. none of these

___ 7. Which of the following is **not** an element of effective planning?

a. goals and objectives

b. motivation

c. processes

d. activities and lessons

e. assessment and evaluation

___ 8. The novice teacher

a. focuses on detailed, written plans and gathering resources.

b. uses a limited repertoire of teaching strategies.

c. attends to children's performance and interests.

d. a and b

e. all of the above

___ 9. The use of holidays as an approach to plan themes, is **not** a good idea **for all but one** of the following reasons, according to Dr. Kostelnik.

a. Holiday themes are often little more than a backdrop for classroom decorations.

b. The resources for teaching holidays are overwhelming and it is difficult to select activities.

c. Children can learn holiday lore and home and in their community.

d. Religious or cultural significance may be lost or trivialized.

___ 10. All of the following are differences between projects and thematic units, **except**

a. time spent on inquiry.

b. outcomes.

c. change yearly.

d. the teacher as an active learner.

## TRUE/FALSE

___ 1. Good planning at every level is a guide that connects meaningful curriculum experiences to the overall goals of a program or school district.

___ 2. Planning begins before the school year and ends on the last day of school.

_____ 3. When you are responsive to the wide range of abilities and learning styles of children in your classroom, you demonstrate to the children that accepting and responding to differences are important democratic values.

_____ 4. An important goal for beginning teachers and others who want to improve their teaching and enable children's learning is to build a repertoire of activities which are easily adapted.

_____ 5. Planning connects classroom learning to the children's community through good use of resources and children's culture.

_____ 6. Planning of experienced teachers is a poor guide for substitute teachers.

_____ 7. The goal of a project is to learn more about a topic by applying higher-level thinking skills.

_____ 8. Projects are a collaborative effort between teacher and learner.

_____ 9. Activity and lesson plans are the same thing.

_____ 10. To achieve the best outcomes for children's learning and development, practitioners must be knowledgeable about and skilled in the various techniques of planning.

SHORT ANSWER

a.  Compare and contrast thematic units and projects. Why are themes and projects used by teachers in planning?

b.      What are the benefits for children of effective planning by teachers?

# *Answers*

## Chapter Review

- environment, transitions, interests (p. 227)
- content, topics; sequence, time (p. 228)
    - ► flexible
    - ► daily, weekly;
    - ► alternatives (p. 228)

- goals, methods; setting the pace, evaluating, assessing (p. 229)
- 4. know, want, learned; 5. reflect (p. 246)

- large group, small group, one-on-one interaction, individual (p. 249)
- build a repertoire with multiple instructional strategies (p. 251)
    - ► Six of the twelve listed on page 252

- The text on pages 253 - 54 provide possible answers.
- 4. assessment (p. 255)
- webbing (p. 255)
- thematic units; projects (p. 255)
- core (p. 259)
- getting started; field work; culminating and debriefing events (p. 261)

**Key terms**

| | | | | | |
|---|---|---|---|---|---|
| 1. D | 2. G | 3. J | 4. K | 5. I | 6. B |
| 7. L | 8. E | 9. F | 10. C | 11. A | 12. H |

## Quick Self Check

Multiple Choice

| | | | | |
|---|---|---|---|---|
| 1. a | 2. e | 3. d | 4. e | 5. e |
| 6. e | 7. b | 8. d | 9. b | 10. d |

True/False

1. T  2. F  3. T  4. F  5. T  6. F  7. T  8. T  9. F  10. T

Short answer

a.  See pages 255 - 263. Themes involve a variety of planned learning experiences around a core concept, whereas projects are in-depth investigations of a topic. Both are used in planning to organize and integrate the curriculum across subject and/or developmental domains. The goal of a project is to learn more about a topic and enhance higher-level thinking skills. Themes help children make connections. Themes usually are a means of managing diverse ability levels and interests of a group of individual children. Projects are learner-initiated and may involve an individual, a small group, or the entire class.

b.  See pages 251 - 52, particularly Figure 7.11, which lists the various functions of planning. Benefits include providing the total picture for the instructional program, using time wisely and productively, asking higher-order questions, empowers one's teaching.

# Chapter Eight

## EXPLORING YOUR ROLE IN DOCUMENTING CHILDREN'S LEARNING

---

*Chapter Review...*

### Chapter Learning Outcomes

- Examine assessment issues and practices affecting young children.
- Understand the purposes of assessment and delineate ways of sharing assessment information with families.
- Develop skills for observing, recording, and analyzing information about children's learning and development.
- Identify and describe the principles of performance assessment.
- Understand the components of a balanced assessment program.

### Chapter Summary

- Assessment in early childhood is defined by NAEYC as "the process of observing, recording, and otherwise documenting the work children do, as a basis for a variety of educational decisions that affect the child."
  - Assessment should not be used to _____.

---

**PAUSE AND REFLECT ABOUT**     *MISCONCEPTIONS ABOUT EARLY CHILDHOOD ASSESSMENT*

1.  What ideas do you have about assessment?

2.  Is it possible that your ideas reflect those of the general public rather than those of a professional educator?

3.  Read the *Ask the Expert* feature on page 278, then make a list of misconceptions that you now hold. After reading the chapter, check your list and consider how the newly acquired information has affected your thinking.

---

- The four main purposes of assessment in early childhood are:
  1.

  2.

  3.

  4.

- Effective early childhood educators have a commitment to equity and fairness that forms the foundations for assessment practices. Competence in a number of areas are needed, including

  ‣ How will you recognize unethical, illegal or otherwise inappropriate use of assessment information?

  ‣ In selecting and developing appropriate assessment methods, one must consider _____ _____, _____ of _____ and the corresponding methods.

  ‣ Administering, scoring, and interpreting the results of various assessment methods.

  ‣ Using _____ assessment data to make decisions about individual students, instructional planning, curriculum development, and programing.

  ‣ _____ assessment results to students, parents, educators, and other audiences.

  ‣ Involving _____ and _____ in the assessment processes. The IEP or _____ _____ _____ and the IFSP or_____ _____ _____ _____ are examples of goal setting by practitioners and families.

- One of the roles of an early childhood practitioner is to make certain that assessment is ongoing, comprehensive, and put to good use. The four major assessment roles early childhood practitioners involve evaluating:
  ‣ learning environment
  ‣ _____ work
  ‣ _____ effectiveness
  ‣ _____ _____.

- Criterion-referenced and norm-referenced tests, two approaches to assessment, have advantages and limitations. Complete the two charts below with the purposes, advantages and disadvantages of each.

►        Another name for a norm-referenced test is _____test.

## Norm-referenced or standardized tests

| Purposes | Advantages | Limitations |
|---|---|---|
| - _____and categorize people<br><br>- measure _____ of students<br><br>- determine _____ objectively | - _____<br><br>- inexpensive<br><br>- _____<br><br>- viewed by public as objective | - provides ____ guidance in _____ instruction<br><br>- over-reliance on single test for decision-making<br><br>- used to _____ children<br><br>- high probability for errors in assessing performance and potential<br><br>- young children do not understand testing procedures<br><br>- problems with _____ validity |

## Criterion-referenced Tests

| Purposes | Advantages | Limitations |
|---|---|---|
| – analyze individual's attainment of _____<br><br>– provide _____ profiles | -- improves _____<br><br>– provides _____ perspectives on learning<br><br>-- is _____<br><br>– invites family and community participation<br><br>– enables critical analysis of curriculum and instruction<br><br>– supports _____ | – time _____<br><br>– expensive<br><br>– requires _____ for educators to use<br><br>– public unfamiliar with this measure and how to understand the results |

●       Assessment in early childhood must be fair, focus on what children can do, examine a range of behaviors, and optimize every child's learning potential.

- The challenge of assessment is to balance traditional means of assessment with performance-based methods of evaluation.

- The seven principles of performance assessment are:
  1. Establish clear performance _____ that state what you expect children to have learned.
  2. Strive for products and performances that relate to the _____ _____.
  3. Publicize _____ and performance standards.
  4. Provide _____ of excellence.
  5. Teach strategies explicitly.
  6. Provide _____ to learners and enable them to make _____.
  7. _____ and celebrate progress.

- Evaluation of _____ _____ _____ and the _____ _____ are the two categories of performance assessment.

- The process of observation includes _____, description followed by _____.
  ▸ Three methods of observation include:
    1.
    2.
    3.
  ▸ To facilitate observation, remember to ...
    ✓ write just enough to jog your memory later
    ✓ keep objective descriptions of behavior separate from subjective interpretations
    ✓ keep materials handy for writing anecdotes.

  ▸ The seven errors to be aware of during observation include: 1) being overly judgmental, 2) overgeneralizing, 3) labeling, 4) _____, 5) _____, 6) making long-term predictions, and 7) _____ children to peers and adults.
  ▸ Some of the benefits of student work portfolios include:
    a. Insight into complex, interactive learning experiences
    b. Provide a _____ for the organization and recording of children's progress

129

c. Show the advantages of relevant learning experiences.

d. Enable the teacher to understand children's _____.

e. Aid in planning for instruction

**PAUSE AND REFLECT ABOUT**      *SYSTEMS OF ASSESSMENT*

1. In most classrooms today, teachers continue to use folders, files, and paperwork to gather assessment information. Read the *Ask the Expert* feature on page 298, then search the Internet for information about computer systems for storing student work portfolios. What systems do you expect to have in place by the time you are finished with your teacher preparation program?

2. List at least 2 web site addresses and summarize the information from each.

    a)



    b)

- Program evaluation focuses on the effectiveness and quality of a program. The question answered by program evaluation is:

_____ ?

  ‣ _____ is the process of displaying children's work on a project with the goal of
    - enhancing children's learning
    - respecting children's ideas and work
    - involving children in the planning and evaluation
    - fostering parent participation
    - making learning process visible.

  ‣ To evaluate a program's quality, five perspectives should be considered:
    - top-down          easily observed and measured characteristics
    - bottom-up          from the child's daily experience
    - _____          working conditions experienced by teachers
    - outside-inside          relationship between staff and families
    - _____          relationships among educational program, the community and the larger social context.

130

- In a balanced early childhood assessment program, teachers realize that learning is far more complex than memorizing information.

- The indicators of a balanced assessment program are:
  - Student motivation to learn.
  - Child and family participation in assessment.
  - Recognition that _____ are part of the learning process.
  - Provision of varied opportunities for children to demonstrate what they have learned.
  - Recognition of the _____ of measurement.
  - Does not confuse _____ with curriculum and instruction.

# Activities . . .

## Key Terms

```
 1.  _ _ _ _ _ _ _ _ A_ _ _   _ _ _ _ _ _ _ _ _ _
 2.          _ _ _ C_ _ _ _ _ _
 3.          _ C_ _ _ _ _ _ _ _ _
 4.         _ O_ _ _ _ _ _ _ _
 5.         _ U_ _ _ _ _ _ _
 6.    _ _ _ _  _ _ _ _ _ _ N_ _ _
 7.        _ T_ _ _ _ _ _ _ _ _
 8.   _ _ _ _ _ _ _ _ _ _ _ A_ _ _ _ _ _ _
 9.        _ _ B_ _ _ _
10.      _ _ _ _ _ _ _ _ I_ _ _
11.     _ _ _ _ _ _ _ - L_ _ _  _ _ _ _ _ _ _ _ _ _
12.      _ _ _ _ _ _ _ _ _ I_ _ _
13.       _ _ _ _ _ _ _ _ _ T_
14. _ _ _ _ _ _ _  _ _ _ _ _ _ _ Y
```

## Clues

1. an assessment approach, in which children are called upon to produce something rather than select the correct answer from several choices and invited to complete tasks that are likely to be encountered outside the classroom (Hamayan, 1995)
2. short, written descriptions of behavior and events
3. tests that analyze in detail each child's attainment of objectives that are deemed reasonable and appropriate for the child
4. purposeful collections of children's work that document achievements and provide data on the processes involved in the products

5.   another term for performance assessment, because of emphasis on practical application of skills

6.   a sample of behavior in a particular domain, which compare the scores of children tested with a reference peer group's performance

7.   another name for # 6

8.   another term for performance assessment because it is a departure from traditional testing methods

9.   refers to scoring using a detailed rating scale

10.  refers to watching learners in action, recording significant details, interpreting the results, and using the data to guide and inform decisions

11.  refers to the child, the family, and the teacher meeting to discuss goals, to review progress, and to make plans for achieving new goals, which is often part of the portfolio process

12.  means that a teacher's performance is judged, not merely by words and actions, but also by the effects of one's teaching on learners

13.  "the process of observing, recording, and documenting the work children do and how they do it, as a basis for a variety of educational decisions that affect the child." (Bredekamp & Rosegrant, 1992, p. 22)

14.  means that a clear connection exists between what is taught and what is assessed

## Project Suggestion

Obtain and read a copy of NAEYC's "Position Statement on Standardized Testing of Young Children 3 Through 8 Years of Age." Write a summary of the position statement. How will information in the statement influence you as an early childhood practitioner?

## Application Activities

❖   *Featuring Families*: When assessment methods differ from those with which the family is familiar, questions arise. In this feature, the teacher focuses on assessment during the Back-to-School Night discussion with parents and responds to parent's concerns.

   ◆   What was your reaction to the conversation? Is it realistic?

   ◆   What perspectives were evident?

♦   Do you think the teacher was successful in her responses?  Explain.


♦   What do you think will happen after the first grading period?


❖   *One Child, Three Perspectives*: Read this feature in your text on pages 304 - 305. The perspectives of a preschool program director, a visiting professor and the classroom aide are presented as they focus on the behavior and needs of a drug-exposed preschooler, Damien.  Respond to the *React, Research, and Reflect* questions.

♦   *React*   In what ways are the perspectives of the program director, the visiting professor, and the aide in the class alike?


♦   *Research*   Investigate the subject of prenatal drug exposure and identify the major issues and recommendations.


What beliefs did the adults in this situation seem to be acting upon?  How did their responses to Damien compare with the recommendations you found?


♦   *Reflect*   Which perspective do you identify most strongly with and why?

## *Journal Entry*

After reading the *Meet the Teachers* segment in this chapter about three different types of assessment, respond to the following questions

*Compare:*    What are some of the commonalities among the assessment practices of these three educators, even though the first is focused on a single child, the second on her overall assessment practices, and the third on a school wide program?

*Contrast:*    How do these educators think about assessment? How would you characterize the outlook of each one?

*Connect:*    What made the greatest impression on you and how will you incorporate this into your teaching?

How do these scenarios compare with your assessment experiences in school?

How has your view of assessment changed?

## Chapter 8 Observation

Interview an early childhood practitioner to determine the forms of evaluation and assessment that are used within the program and the reasons for the types and methods used. Use the form below and enter your questions and the practitioner's response.  If possible, request a copy of any assessment/ evaluation forms the teacher may use.

Teacher's name_____ Date of interview_____

School/program name:_____

Age group/grade taught:_____

Questions

- How do you assess the children's progress in your class?

- 

- 

- 

-

## Authentic Assessment

Select a learner age level: infant, toddler, preschool, kindergarten, 1st-3rd grade. Then write a goal for each of the major developmental domains - physical, social, emotional, cognitive. For each goal, describe two methods of assessment appropriate for the goal and the age level. Part of the description will include a sample of the recording technique used to document the behavior, skill, or ability. Use the following form to summarize your work.

## *Resources . . .*

### Videos and other audio-visual materials...

*Charting Growth – Assessment (30 min).* National Association for the Education of Young Children (NAEYC)

*Looking at Young Children. (1988) (16 min.).* University of Minnesota; Audio-Visual Library Services.

*Performance Assessment: A Teacher's Way of Knowing (30 min.).* DavidsonFilms.

*Windows on Learning: A Framework for Making Decisions (20 min.).* NAEYC.

### Additional Reading...

Bredekamp, S. & Rosegrant (Eds.) (1995). *Reaching potentials: Appropriate curriculum and assessment for young children, Vol.1.* Washington, DC: NAEYC.

Culbertson, L. D. & Jalongo, M. R. (1999). "But what's wrong with letter grades?" Responding to parents' questions about assessment. *Childhood Education, 75*(3), 130 - 135.

Grace, C. & Shores, F.E. (1991). *The Portfolio and Its Use: Developmentally Appropriate Assessment of Young Children.* Little Rock, AR: Southern Early Childhood Association (SECA).

Granlund, G. (1998). Portfolios as an assessment tool: Is collection of work enough? *Young Children 53*(3), 4 - 10.

Haladyna, T., Haas, N. & Allison, J. (1998). Continuing tensions in standardized testing. *Childhood Education 74*(5), 262 - 273.

Hartman, J.A. & Eckerty, C. (1995). Projects in the early years. *Childhood Education 71*, 141-48.

Helm, J.H., Beneke, S., & Steinheimer, K. (1998). *Windows on Learning: Documenting Young Children's Work*, New York: Teachers College Press.

Mayfield, P.K. & Chapman, J.K. (1998). Children's prenatal exposure to drugs: Implications for early childhood educators. *Dimensions of Early Childhood 26(3-4)*, 38-42.

Meisels, S.J. (1995). *Developmental screening in early childhood: A guide (4th ed.),* Washington, DC: NAEYC.

Southern Early Childhood Association (1995). *Developmentally Appropriate Assessment.* A position statement. Little Rock: AR: Author.

Taylor, J. (1999). Child-led parent/school conferences–In second grade?!?, *Young Children 54*(1), 78-82.

Weldin, D.J. & Tumarkin, S. R. (1999). Parent involvement – More power in the portfolio process. *Childhood Education 74*(2), 90-95.

Name_____

Learner Age Level:_____

### Physical
Goal:

Assessment # 1:

Assessment # 2:

### Social
Goal:

Assessment # 1:

Assessment # 2:

### Emotional
Goal:

Assessment # 1:

Assessment # 2:

### Cognitive
Goal:

Assessment # 1:

Assessment # 2:

# *Quick Self Check*

MULTIPLE CHOICE

___ 1. The purposes of assessment for children and families include all the following **except**
   a.   to assess the value or worth of a program.
   b.   to make decisions about support services for children.
   c.   to obtain feedback on ways to improve teaching.
   d.   to help children build self-evaluation skills.

___ 2. The best way for teachers to show children's efforts and progress to parents and the community is
   a.   a portfolio of information gathered over time.
   b.   a test score or grade in statistical terms.
   c.   a parent-teacher conference.
   d.   none of these

___ 3. To meet the multiple assessment roles in early childhood, the practitioner must
   a.   practice strict confidentiality.
   b.   treat all children the same.
   c.   be fair and equitable.
   d.   a and c

___ 4. Some of the disadvantages of norm-referenced testing include
   a.   comparing and categorizing people.
   b.   using a single test score to make a decision.
   c.   making significant errors in assessing young children's performance and potential.
   d.   b and c

___ 5. A _____ is the assessment approach that is very detailed, is more time-consuming, and is not generally accepted by the public.
   a.   norm-referenced test
   b.   criterion-referenced assessment
   c.   standardized test
   d.   student work portfolio

___ 6. _____ is when children are called upon to produce something and are invited to complete tasks that relate to the real world outside the classroom.
   a.   Performance assessment
   b.   Alternative assessment
   c.   Authentic assessment
   d.   all of these

___ 7. The purposes of observation include the following **except**
   a.    to plan the curriculum.
   b.    to watch the children play.
   c.    to make referrals.
   d.    to learn a child's interests and abilities.

___ 8. _____ is a method of observing and recording, which charts information that record yes/no or absence/presence of a behavior.
   a.    Checklist
   b.    Anecdotal record
   c.    Rating scale
   d.    Event sampling

___ 9. _____ is a major error in observation that characterizes someone's entire personality with a word.
   a.    Overgeneralizing
   b.    Stereotyping
   c.    Labeling
   d.    Blaming

___ 10. To determine if an assessment program is balanced and working well, a practitioner would consider all of the following **except**
   a.    Students' motivation to learn.
   b.    Child and family participation in assessment.
   c.    Failure to recognize the limitations of measurement.
   d.    Variety of opportunities for children to demonstrate what they have learned.

## TRUE/FALSE

___ 1. Assessment should help inform instructional decisions, result in benefits for the child and family, and relate to what the child is learning in school.

___ 2. As an early childhood professional, one must guard against sharing professional information in unprofessional ways with colleagues and other members of the community.

___ 3. Young children are excellent paper-and-pencil test takers.

___ 4. Virtually all standardized tests emphasize verbal skills only.

___ 5. In early childhood, the range of abilities that is evaluated through traditional tests is a major limitation of testing.

___ 6. The challenge in assessment is to balance traditional means of assessment with performance-based methods of assessment.

___ 7. According to Dr. Leong technology will hinder the early childhood practitioner's assessment of children in the future.

___ 8. Documentation is the process of displaying children's work on a class project.

___ 9. When dealing with program evaluation, the outside-inside perspective deals with the relationship between the educational program, the community, and the larger social context in which it operates.

___10. Teacher accountability means that practitioner performance is judged not by the effects of one's teaching on learners, but by simple words and actions.

## SHORT ANSWER

1. Discuss the relationship between assessment and instruction.

2. Compare and contrast assessment and testing.

# *Answers*

## Chapter Summary

- label children

- 1. Plan instruction for individuals and groups of children; 2. Communicate with families; 3. Identify children and families; 4. Evaluate quality and effectiveness (p. 277)
- Confidentiality is of upmost importance in the use of assessment methods and information. (p. 280)
  - ▶ children's rights; purposes, assessment (p. 280)
  - ▶ comprehensive;
  - ▶ communicating (p. 281);
  - ▶ children, families (p. 282); Individualized Educational Plan, Individualized Family Service Plan (p. 282)
- children's, program, professional performance (p. 285)

- standardized (p.286)

### *Norm-referenced or standardized tests*

| Purposes | Advantages | Limitations |
|---|---|---|
| - compare and categorize people<br><br>- measure performance of students<br><br>- determine opportunities objectively | - efficient<br><br>- inexpensive<br><br>- convenient<br><br>- viewed by public as objective | - provide no guidance in planning instruction<br><br>- over-reliance on single test for decision-making<br><br>- used to label children<br><br>- high probability for errors in assessing performance and potential<br><br>- young children do not understand testing procedures<br><br>- problems with content validity |

141

*Criterion-referenced Tests*

| Purposes | Advantages | Limitations |
|---|---|---|
| – analyze individual's attainment of objectives<br><br>– provide individual profiles | – improves learning<br><br>– provides multiple perspectives on learning<br><br>– is systematic<br><br>– invites family and community participation<br><br>– enables critical analysis of curriculum and instruction<br><br>– supports collaboration | – time consuming<br><br>– expensive<br><br>– requires training for educators to use<br><br>– public unfamiliar with this measure and how to understand the results |

(pp. 286 - 289)

- 1. targets, 2. real world, 3. criteria, 4. models, 6. feedback, adjustments, 7. document (p. 289)
- individual children's progress, overall program (p. 291)
- perceptions, interpretations;
  - ▸ time sampling, anecdotal records, specimen record, event sampling, checklists, rating scales, audio, video or photograph, interviews, children's drawings (p. 292)
  - ▸ 4) stereotyping, 5) blaming (p. 294); 7) comparing (p. 295)
  - ▸ b. framework (p. 299)

  - ▸ d. abilities (p. 299)
- "Am I providing a quality program?" (p. 299)
  - ▸ documentation (p. 299);
  - ▸ inside, outside (p.300)

- 3. errors (p. 301); 5. limitations; 6. measurement (p. 302)

## Key terms

1. performance assessment(p. 289)
2. anecdotes (p. 291)
3. criterion-referenced tests (p. 288)
4. portfolios (pp. 293-94)
5. authentic assessment (p. 289)
6. norm-referenced tests (p. 286)
7. standardized (p. 286)
8. alternative assessment (p. 289)
9. rubric (p. 288)
10. observation (p. 291)
11. student-led conference (p. 282)
12. teacher accountability
13. assessment (p. 277)
14. content validity (p. 288)

142

## Quick Self Check

**Multiple Choice**

| | | | | |
|---|---|---|---|---|
| 1. c | 2. a | 3. d | 4. d | 5. b |
| 6. d | 7. b | 8. a | 9. c | 10. c |

**True/False**

1. T    2. T    3. F    4. F    5. T    6. T    7. F    8. T    9. F    10. F

**Short answer**

a.      See p. 278. Information gained from assessment should have a direct influence on planning for specific children and groups of children as it provides information about what children know and are able to do, as well as what their strengths and weaknesses are. Observation as an assessment tool also provides insight into how learning was enhanced or hindered by the planned curriculum experiences.

b.      Testing is a means of measurement. It is one type of assessment tool. The current view of assessment is based on a broader view of what assessment should do. See p. 288. Compare the results from testing with those obtained from authentic assessment (pages 285 - 291).

# Chapter Nine

# EXPLORING YOUR ROLE IN GUIDING CHILDREN'S BEHAVIOR

## Chapter Review...

### Chapter Learning Outcomes

- Learn the components necessary in developing a classroom that is a community of learners.

- Understand children's rights and needs and the ways in which those rights and needs shape a child guidance philosophy.

- Become aware of the effects of a violent society on the development of young children.

- Understand aggressive behavior in children and appropriate responses to it.

- Define conflict, common types of conflict, and ways to resolve conflict in the classroom.

- Develop greater confidence in your ability to function as a mediator and teach children self-control.

- Acquire more skillful ways of communicating with children when difficult issues arise.

### Chapter Summary

- Children's needs and rights are fundamental in understanding misbehavior and in developing guidance strategies.
  - The primary right of children is to have _____ _____.
  - Basic needs include freedom from threat, adequate rest, shelter, _____, and _____.
  - Fundamental personal and social needs include (a) _____, (b) _____,(c) _____, and hope.
  - According to Glasser (1992) the four fundamental motivations for behavior are:
    1.
    2.
    3.
    4.

- ▸ Although young children generally strive to please adults, when misbehavior occurs, there are four possible underlying causes:
  1. Physical environment
  2. Children's basic needs are unmet
  3. _____ _____
  4. Cultural differences

- When a child misbehaves, one needs to consider whether what is expected is _____, productive, _____, and age appropriate (Kohn, 1996).

---

**PAUSE AND REFLECT ABOUT          DISCIPLINE**

- • "All of you will sit here and miss recess until the person who broke the rules comes forward."
- • "If everyone gets 100% on the spelling test on Friday, we will have a popcorn party."
- • "You know the rules. Now you have to write 'I will not throw snowballs' 500 times."
- • "I like the way that Heather is working. Look a Heather's picture, everyone."

1. Which of the above did you experience as a child?

2. How did you feel about such statements?

3. What connections do you see between these statements and the children's rights listed in Figure 9.1 on page 313?

---

- One of the great fallacies of working with young children is the assumption that whatever adults say is appropriate and the role of the child is to _____.

- Guiding young children's behavior requires establishing and maintaining a relationship and effective communication. Some of the behaviors which demonstrate effective communication are to:
  - ▸ identify with the child's situation
  - ▸ use a pleasant, calm, and normal tone of voice
  - ▸ state expectations in a clear, simple, polite, firm, and _____way
  - ▸ offer _____ suggestions and alternatives for behavior

- ▸ enjoy and verbally _____ children's appropriate behavior
- ▸ express feelings in an appropriate and constructive manner
- ▸ use humor
- ▸ be _____ and predictable
- ▸ use positive _____ communication such as smiles

---

**PAUSE AND REFLECT ABOUT**    *AGGRESSIVE TODDLERS–WHAT ARE THEY TELLING US?*

Read the segment on page 320 and watch the video segment. Then answer the following questions.

1.    Which of the children's rights as listed in Figure 9.1 (p. 313) are being addressed by the solutions presented in this video segment?

2.    List three options for dealing with a child's aggressive behavior when the parent is present, but seems to be ignoring the behavior. How are these options different from the ways you would deal with a child's behavior when a parent is not present?
   a.

   b.

   c.

---

- ● Many experts are expressing concern about the escalation of violence in children's lives.

- ● One of the most important things that any adult responsible for the care and education of young children can do is to try and prevent behavior problems before they occur. Prevention strategies include:
  - ▸ Know children's _____ and _____.
  - ▸ Have a well-organized classroom and clearly established routines.
  - ▸ Discuss rules and _____.
  - ▸ Teach, _____, and _____ appropriate behaviors.
  - ▸ Avoid reinforcing the wrong sort of behavior.
  - ▸ Think before you speak.
  - ▸ Choose your _____.
  - ▸ Use children's literature.

- Aggression concerns most teachers, however research on children's aggressive behavior reveals that:
    1. Aggression is in the eye of the beholder.
    2. Child behavior that disrupts ongoing play and elicits negative responses usually leads to even stronger feelings of isolation, anxiety, and hostility.
    3. Teachers focus on individual children who are aggressive, when it would be more effective to work with the total group.
    4. Aggressive behavior frequently occurs in _____.
    5. Aggressive acts occur _____ frequently than teachers assume.
    6. Sometimes teachers intervene too quickly when aggression occurs.

- Teachers need to encourage children to use their own problem-solving resources rather than playing the role of referee.

- There is a child guidance continuum which ranges from least intrusive to most intrusive. Two "least intrusive" strategies include:
    1.
    2.
    Two "most intrusive" strategies are:
    1.
    2.

- Six basic precepts of teaching children to get along with each other are:
    1. Identify with the _____, not the _____.
    2. Focus on the child's needs rather than fear of failure.
    3. When confronted with the most difficult teaching situations go back to the basics - sensory experiences, _____, and _____.
    4. Don't expect that you can make it all better.
    5. Follow the _____ _____.
    6. Learn how to talk with children about inappropriate behavior.

- Social conflict does not belong to a child; it is a consequence of relationships.
    ‣ Experts on conflict resolution have identified three main outcomes of conflict:
        1.
        2.
        3.
    ‣ Recent brain research suggests that the _____ environments built by teachers in the classroom exert a powerful influence on _____.

    ▸    A classroom community is an approach to positive social environments.

- Methods of early childhood conflict resolution are grounded in the belief that if teachers guide the young child in learning to feel empowered, then the need to do unkind things is decreased.

  ▸    List the eight basic types of conflicts.
  1.    Possession disputes
  2.    _____ _____
  3.    _____ struggles
  4.    Personality clashes
  5.    Group-entry disputes
  6.    Aggressive play
  7.    Teasing and _____ _____
  8.    Shifting _____

---

**PAUSE AND REFLECT ABOUT**    *CHILDREN'S NEED TO FEEL SIGNIFICANT*

Now that you have examined Beaty's eight different types of conflict that typically occur in classrooms (pages 331 - 36), try to explain how each one is a child's effort to say, in effect, "I am important."

---

- When guiding children to appropriate behavior, skillful teachers
  - separate the behavior from the child,
  - are objective, and
  - do not take the misbehavior personally.

- Although teachers usually view conflict with apprehension, Beaty (1995) suggests that conflict can be be viewed as an opportunity to learn about one's self in relationship to others.

# Activities...

## Key Terms

### Across

2. refers to competing wishes, desires, or behaviors that evoke powerful emotions

4. refers to the response to children's misbehavior

5. refers to any deliberate act that is designed to harm or diminish another person in some way

8. an outcome of a conflict in which agreement is reached through negotiation

9. type of violence that refers to the injuries children suffer from abuse or neglect, as well as violent acts children witness between and among adults or family members

10. unpleasant or painful experiences that are imposed upon others to enforce compliance

11. an outcome of conflict in which one side is victorious over the other

### Down

1. on-going process of managing children's behavior based on the types of adults society hopes children will become

2. physical pain, such as spanking, inflicted to force compliance

3. type of violence that refers to the aggressive acts children see depicted, such as in television, videos, and magazines

6. type of violence children witness within their neighborhoods, such as shootings, fights, and stabbings

7. an outcome of conflict in which no one feels like the loser in the dispute and everyone wins

## Project Suggestions

a.  Brainstorm behavior management situations with others in your class. Be sure to include size of class, age of children, number of adults working with the children. Then if your instructor has arranged an in-class experience with a panel of practitioners to discuss their approaches to guidance and to respond to questions from students about how to handle different problems, select by consensus those situations to which the panelists will be asked to respond. An alternative would be to select two early childhood practitioners and interview each teacher using one of the scenarios as the basis of the interview. Then prepare a brief report comparing the similarities and contrasting the differences between the two teachers' responses.

## Application activities

❖  *Meet the Teachers*     Read about how Charles, Mrs. Davis, and Ms. Pettit handle child guidance on pages 309-310. Then respond to the *Compare/ Contrast/Connect* questions.

*Compare:*     What are some of the commonalities among these three teachers, even though they are working with children of various ages?

*Contrast:*     How do these teachers think about teaching? How would you characterize the outlook of each one?

*Connect:*     What made the greatest impression on you, and how will you incorporate this into your teaching?

❖ *Ask the Expert*    Read Edyth Wheeler's discussion of conflict resolution on pages 340 - 42.

♦ What does "constructive conflict" mean?

♦ What skills do children learn from conflict?

♦ Describe Dr. Wheeler's framework for creating a caring classroom.

❖ *Featuring Families*    This feature, on pages 337 - 38, illustrates two different responses to a conflict and what the children involved may have learned from each response. Developing the skills of conflict resolution require practitioners to become aware of what they say and its potential influence on young children. Choose 3 of the statements on page 345 and write what the comment may have taught the child. If you are not satisfied with the statement, provide an alternative, and then consider what the child may have learned.

1.

2.

3.

## *Journal Entry*

Read about Earl's disruptive behavior in the *One Child, Three Perspectives* feature on pages 243 - 44. Then respond to the following *React/Research/Reflect* questions.

♦ **React**       In what ways are the perspectives of these adults alike? How do their approaches to meet Earl's needs vary?

♦ **Research**       Read several articles in the library about young children with difficult family circumstances, such as homelessness, poverty, urban violence. What recommendations were made?

♦ **Reflect**       What might be the underlying reasons for the differences in the responses to Earl's situation? Which perspective do you identify most strongly with, and why?

## Chapter 11  Observation

Observe for at least 45 minutes in an early childhood classroom.  During that time, note each guidance or management approach that is used with the children by any adult present in the classroom.  These may be interventions taken by the teacher or preparations of the environment or actions of the children that indicate they have participated previously in some planned arrangement.  Then prepare a graph using the continuum from the text and indicate the frequency of the various techniques noted in the observation.  What conclusions may be drawn?

## Authentic Assessment

a.  Respond to these two questions and then include the responses in a section of your portfolio labeled Classroom Management:.

(1) Describe why it is important for a teacher to maintain authority in the classroom and describe several ways in which you would establish your authority as a beginning teacher. How would you balance your own authority with children's need for autonomy? Provide several examples.

(2) Describe the role of the practitioner/teacher planning on the guidance process. What behavior problems can be avoided through adequate planning and why?

b.      The following activity may also serve as a special project for this chapter. Develop an article file on discipline/child guidance. Collect five articles from popular media, such as *Parent Magazine and Family Circle,* and five articles from professional journals, such as *Instructor* and *Young Children*. For each of the articles in the file, complete the following form and attach a completed copy to the article.

Article title:

Article's author:_____

Publication name:_____

     Date of publication:_____ Vol._____ No._____ Pages_____

Critique (2-3 paragraphs on the content, the appropriateness of the technique(s) suggested, and for whom the article may be helpful).

# Resources...

## Videos and other audio-visual materials...

*The Art of Communication (1986). (30 min.).* Insight Media.

*Discipline: Appropriate Guidance of Young Children (28 min.).* National Association for the Education of Young Children (NAEYC).

*Discipline and the Physical Environment (25 min.).* Distributed by Redleaf Press.

*How Caring Relationships Support Self-Regulation (68 min.).* NAEYC.

*How Do I Tell You I Like You? (1990) (19 min.).* Creative Educational Video.

*How to Talk So Kids Will Listen (1988) (6 segments-30 min. each).* Insight Media.

*"Relating to Others" (1991)-* video # 3 in *Raising America's Children.*

## Additional Reading...

Bauer, K. L. & Sheerer, M.A. (1997 September). Creative strategies in Earnie's early childhood classroom, *Young Children 52*(6), 47 - 52.

Crockenberg, S. (1992 April). How children learn to resolve conflicts in families, *Zero to Three,* 11 - 13.

DaRoss, D. A. & Kovach, L. J. (1998). Assisting toddlers and caregivers during conflict resolutions: Interactions that promote socializations, *Childhood Education, 75*(1), 25 - 30.

Gordon, A. & Browne, K. (1996). *Guiding Young Children in a Diverse Society.* Needham Heights, MA: Allyn & Bacon.

Hewitt, D. (1995). *So This Is Normal Too?* St. Paul, MN: Redleaf Press.

Katz, L. G. & McClellan, D. E. (1997). *Fostering Children's Social Competence: The Teacher's Role.* Washington, DC: National Association for the Education of Young Children.

Paley, V. G. (1992). *You Can't Say You Can't Play.* Cambridge, MA: Harvard University Press.

Thompson, S. (1997 September). Helping primary children with recess play: A social curriculum. *Young Children, 52*(6),17-21.

# Quick Self Check

MULTIPLE CHOICE

___ 1. The first and most important right of children is
    a.     that basic human needs for food and shelter are met.
    b.     to have caring relationships.
    c.     to be treated with respect and dignity.
    d.     to have hope of a brighter future.

___ 2. All of the following are underlying causes of children's behavior **except**
    a.     the physical environment.
    b.     special needs.
    c.     basic needs are met.
    d.     cultural differences

___ 3. Early childhood practitioners should consider which of the following questions when a child misbehaves.
    a.     Is it necessary?
    b.     Is it productive and fair?
    c.     Is it age appropriate?
    d.     All of these

___ 4. _____ helps a child internalize a code of conduct.
    a.     Discipline
    b.     Child guidance
    c.     Praise
    d.     Encouragement

___ 5. All the following are related to praise **except**
    a.     is a private event.
    b.     focuses on outcomes.
    c.     teacher judges what is good or bad.
    d.     children and their work is judged.

___ 6. With virtually every American home having a television set, _____ is a reality in almost every home.
    a.     media violence
    b.     domestic violence
    c.     family violence
    d.     community violence

____ 7. Research on aggressive behavior reveals that
   a.   aggression is in the eye of the beholder.
   b.   some children evidence behavior patterns that result in what they don't need.
   c.   aggression frequently occurs in groups.
   d.   all of these

____ 8. Encouraging children to say what to do in response to misbehavior is a guidance strategy called _____.
   a.   acting as a reporter or narrator
   b.   offering choices
   c.   brainstorming
   d.   offering ideas

____ 9. The best time to gain acceptance from a child is
   a.   during time out.
   b.   when a child is at play.
   c.   during a class meeting.
   d.   none of these

____10. A classroom community is characterized by
   a.   effective communication and dynamic, interactive learning.
   b.   a sense of belonging and opportunities to deal with feelings, ideas, and values.
   c.   agreed upon standards for behavior and fair treatment.
   d.   all of these

TRUE/FALSE

____ 1. The four fundamental motivations for behavior are fun, power, freedom, and love.

____ 2. Rewards are experiences that are imposed on others to "teach a lesson" and enforce compliance.

____ 3. Bribes are warnings about punishments that will occur if the child does not comply with the rules.

____ 4. Poverty is a major risk factor for violence.

____ 5. One of the most important things an early childhood practitioner can do is prevent behavior problems before they occur.

_____ 6. Aggressive acts occur more frequently than teachers assume.

_____ 7. Child behavior that disrupts ongoing play and elicits negative responses usually has no effect on future behavior.

_____ 8. Social conflict is not a consequence of relationships, but belongs to a child.

_____ 9. The basics for young children are sensory experiences, play, and enactment.

_____ 10. The goal of conflict resolution is to promote peace and equity and build a sense of community.


SHORT ANSWER

a.    How does a teacher communicate responsibly to children while using conflict resolution strategies?

b.    Describe the group decision-making process through the example of deciding if the children should play outside after 3 rainy days. Be sure to include the "keys for keeping children engaged."

c.    Describe how praise and encouragement differ and give an example of each not listed in the text.

# *Answers*

## Chapter Review

- caring relationships (p. 311)
  - ▸ food, clothing (p. 311)
  - ▸ 1. autonomy, 2. relatedness, 3. competence (p. 312)

  - ▸ love, power, freedom, or fun (p. 314)
  - ▸ 3. curriculum problems ( p. 314)
- necessary (p. 315); fair (p. 316)
- obey (p. 318)
  - ▸ positive (p. 318)
  - ▸ appropriate (p. 318)

  - ▸ appreciate (p. 318);
  - ▸ consistent
  - ▸ nonverbal (p. 320)
- ▸ abilities, limitations (p.3 22);
  - ▸ consequences,
  - ▸ practice, review;
  - ▸ battles (p. 323)

- groups (p. 324); less (p. 325)
- Any 2 from 1-5; any 2 from 6-10 (p. 326)
- 1. child, label (p. 327); 3. play, enactment; 5. child's lead (p. 328)
- 1. domination, 2. compromise, 3. integration (p. 329)
  - ▸ social; learning (p. 329)

- 2. attention getting (p.332), 3. power (p.333), 7. name calling (p. 335), 8. blame (p. 336)


## Key Terms

### Across
2. conflict (p. 321)
4. discipline (p. 319)
5. aggression (p. 324)
8. compromise (p. 329)
9. family violence (p. 321)
10. punishment (p. 317)
11. domination (p. 329)

### Down
1. guidance (p. 319)
2. corporal punishment (p. 317)
3. media violence (p. 321)
6. community violence (p. 321)
7. conflict resolution (p. 329)

# Quick Self Check

## Multiple Choice

| | | | | |
|---|---|---|---|---|
| 1. b | 2. c | 3. d | 4. b | 5. a |
| 6. a | 7. d | 8. c | 9. b | 10. d |

## True/False

1. T  2. F  3. F  4. T  5. T  6. F  7. F  8. F  9. T  10. T

## Short answer

a.  See pages 318 and 320 for effective communication techniques and blend with the information in the *Ask the Expert* feature on pages 340 - 42.

b.  See page 330 for process.  For the situation, the outcomes of the discussion should arrive at consensus and establish possible consequences for the decision, such as, avoiding muddy sections or play quietly on the patio.

c.  See page 319.  Examples will vary.

# Chapter Ten

## EXPLORING YOUR ROLE IN SUPPORTING FAMILIES

---

## *Chapter Review...*

### Chapter Learning Outcomes

- Be introduced to the parent involvement traditions in the field of early childhood education.
- Examine goals and models of home-school communication, collaboration, and support.
- Recognize the early childhood professional's unique role in promoting home-school collaboration.
- Learn general techniques and practical strategies for building mutual trust and respect with families.
- Apply knowledge of school-community partnerships to various early childhood settings.
- Identify exemplary practices in parent involvement and model programs for working with families.

### Chapter Summary

- It is essential that early childhood practitioners understand the importance of families for children's_____ and _____ and the changes influencing family life.
  - The characteristics of well-functioning families include:

    | | | | |
    |---|---|---|---|
    | a. | Communication | e. | Shared time |
    | b. | Cohesiveness | f. | Shared _____ |
    | c. | Clear _____ | g. | Social support |
    | d. | _____ | | |

- Early childhood practitioners are *family resource persons*, who build trust and respect between, among, and with families, and the larger community.
  - Your role as a *family resource person* must be governed by interest in

    _____ _____.
  - To be successful in this role, you need to:
    1. Apply knowledge of child development and problem solving when interacting with families.

2. Acknowledge and _____ parents' feelings.
3. Remain focused on both the child's and the group's needs.
4. Maintain a professional demeanor.
5. Form dynamic, supportive _____
   with programs, schools, and community agencies.
6. Begin _____ in the family's life.

● Understanding the family as a social system is important for these three reasons:
   1. Children and parents influence each other as they adapt over time.
   2. Family problems and issues are related to children's development as
      learners.
   3. _____ to the _____ are significant for
      children's and families' well-being.

● Participation in special activities with the community setting provides the bonds
   children and families need for healthy development.

- Although previous parent involvement efforts had limitations, improved home-school relationships are characterized by _____, _____ and _____ _____.

    ▸ Six basic types of involvement building partnerships between schools and families and communities are:
        1.                              4.
        2.                              5.
        3.                              6.

    ▸ Six guidelines for working effectively with families are:
        1.    Be aware that the boundaries separating responsibilities for children are blurring.
        2.    Confront your own _____ about families.
        3.    Recognize the unique position to identify children's needs and initiate families interactions with schools.
        4.    Appreciate the importance of effective _____ and _____ in interactions with families.
        5.    Reach out to _____ and _____.
        6.    Explore many dimensions in working with families and communities.

163

- Families and educators views of a child are different, yet complementary, with each contributing to an understanding of the child, his or her progress, and causes for specific behaviors.

- The obstacles to effective partnerships with parents may be overcome with a variety of strategies.

  ‣ The five barriers, which must be overcome:
      1.
      2.
      3.
      4.
      5.

  ‣ Some "family friendly" ways to achieve partnerships are:
      --    Try to ease families' concerns about children's adjustment.
      –    Keep professional _____ to a minimum.

164

- Make it _____ for the family to stay informed.
- Provide opportunities for families to gather informally and _____ .
- Schedule meetings at various times.
- Use a variety of strategies to communicate with families.
- Strive to identify with and meet the _____ _____ of families.
- Be sensitive to some family members' discomfort in school settings.
- When difficulties arise, keep a problem-solving focus instead of _____.
- Focus on _____ families.
- Allow parents to contribute in their own ways.
- Admit when you need to seek outside assistance.

- Guidelines for making referrals include:
  - Know the services and agencies in your area.
  - Identify competent people in those groups with whom you can work.
  - Make referrals to _____ _____.
  - Secure family members' _____ to participate.
  - Follow up.

- Conferencing with parents or other family members about an individual child are an important component of home-school partnerships and formal conferences include three phases:
  - Preparation before
  - Conducting the conference
  - Following up on a conference

- Although diverse cultures and children with disabilities create teacher concerns, your role as a *family resource person* requires you to view parents as _____ partners in education, support parents' efforts to help children learn at home, _____ for children's basic needs, and be able to _____ families to available resources.

- Family resource or family support programs emphasize support, resources, _____, and meeting individual needs to enhance family life.

  - These programs contrast traditional family programs.
  - Family support needs to be addressed as a _____ _____issue.

- ➤ Three things are needed for social reform: a knowledge base, a social strategy and a _____ _____.

- ● Two reasons for concerns of new practitioners about working with families are:
  1. Initial focus on teaching the child, and
  2. See self as lacking authority with parents because teachers may not be parents.

- ● By working effectively with children, families, and the community at large, early childhood practitioners can make a significant difference in the lives and the learning of the children entrusted to their care.

# Activities . . .

**Key Terms**    Define the following terms from this chapter.

collaboration (p.370): _____

_____

comprehensive service model (p.370): _____

_____

educare (p.356): _____

_____

empowerment (p. 370):_____

_____

family (p.352 ):_____

_____

family involvement (p.356):_____

_____

family resource/support program (pp. 370-71):_____

_____

parent-teacher conference (pp.367-69): _____

_____

**Project Suggestion**
Research websites for early childhood practitioners on family involvement and also websites that would support families.  Compile a list of 5 sites for

practitioners and 5 sites for families with the correct url. For each site, state the name of the site, indicate who sponsors the site, when it was last updated, how accurate you think the information is, and your opinion of the site's usefulness.

Summarize with a paragraph about what you would include in a family support/involvement website and explain your choices.

## Application activities

❖ *Featuring Families*:  Establishing communication with families should begin before the child's first day within a program.  Home visits and questionnaires are two ways of collecting information about a child's family and encouraging participation with a program.  This feature provides one sample of a family questionnaire.  How would you respond if they received such a questionnaire?

If this were a part of a home visit, what additional information would you be interested in?

❖ *One Child, Three Perspectives:* The needs of a very young immigrant and adoptee are viewed from the perspectives of David's mother, his Russian teachers, and his American teachers.  How would you work with a child like David in a classroom?  Read this feature in your text on pages 377-379, then complete the *React/Research/Reflect* questions.

     ◆   **React**       In what ways are the perspectives of David's mother, David's teachers in Russia, and his teachers in America alike?  How do their approaches to meeting David's needs vary?  What might be the underlying reasons for these differences.

♦ **_Research_**  Locate several journal articles on second-language learners who are newly immigrated.  What is recommended by the experts?

♦ **_Reflect_**  Which perspective do you identify most strongly with, and why?

## *Journal Entry*

After reading the *Meet the Teachers* segment on pages 349-350, which provides brief glimpses into how three teachers early childhood teachers responded to the needs of families, respond to the *Compare/Contrast/Connect* questions.

*Compare:*     What are some of the commonalities among these three teachers, even though they are working with different families in different settings?

*Contrast:*     How do these teachers think about families?  How would you characterize the outlook of each one?

Theo Spewock –

Ms. Cole –

Ms. Latall –

*Connect:*     What made the greatest impression on you, and how will you incorporate this view of families into your teaching?

**Chapter 10 Observation**

Attend a meeting of a school board, Head Start Advisory Committee, a parent advisory committee for a preschool or child care program, or a PTA. Observe the proceedings, obtain a copy of the agenda, and try to determine how parents make decisions through these groups. Prepare a brief report on your impressions and what you learned at the meeting that will influence how _you_ interact with parents.

## Authentic Assessment

Using the information in your text, your reflections on parent involvement, and personal experience, respond to the following situation in writing. Your response should include your perception of the situation (or problem) and two ways to respond. Try to anticipate the possible outcomes of each response. References are required.

_Sometimes parents may exhibit hostility toward the school and often the teacher. What would you do if..._
_During a conference, a parent becomes angry with the teacher. She bursts out with the comment, "My daughter never had a problem with any of her other teachers. There must be something wrong with you, if you are having problems with her fighting with other children. Don't tell me what to do. She needs to be able to defend herself. If you ask me, you are the problem. She always got along before."_

# Resources . . .

## Videos and other audio-visual materials...

Cultivating Roots–Home/School Partnerships (28 minutes). NAEYC.

Family Influences (1992). Insight Media

Partnership with Parents (28 minutes). NAEYC.

## Additional Reading...

Beginnings Workshop (1997 July). Parent conferences, _Child Care Information Exchange, 116_, 39-58.

Coleman, M. & Churchill, S. (1997 Spring). Challenges to family involvment, _Childhood Education,73_(3), 144-148.

Enge, N. (1999). Issues in education: "Do I belong here?" Understanding the adopted, language minority child, *Childhood Education, 75*(2), 106-108.

Galinsky, E. (1990). Parents and teachers/caregivers: Sources of tension, sources of support, *Young Children, 43*(3), 4-12.

Hannigan, I. (1998). *Off to School: A Parent's-Eye View of the Kindergarten Year.* Washington, DC: National Association for the Education of Young Children.

McBride, S. L. (1999). Family-centered practices. *Young Children, 54*(3), 62-68.

Stroud, J. E., Stroud, J. C. & Staley, L. M. (1997). Understanding and supporting adoptive families. *Early Childhood Education Journal, 24*(4), 229-234.

Swick, K. J. (1991). *Teacher-Parent Partnerships to Enhance School Success in Early Childhood Programs.* Little Rock, AK: Southern Early Childhood Association.

Swick, K. J. (1993). *Strengthening Parents and Families During the Early Childhood Years.* Washington , DC: National Education Association.

*Web sites:*

www.earlychildhood.com/article.html     Article on Parent-Teacher Conferences by Evelyn Peterson

www.pta.org/programs/edulibr.html     Information and on-line brochures and articles from the national PTA.

www.connectforkids.org     Former site of *Kids Campaign* now sponsoring a Guidance for Grownups program

http://npin.org/     National Parent Information Network includes a section - Resources for those who work with parents and links to other sites

www.udel.edu/batemean/acei/indx.htm    Association for Childhood Education web site - check index or conduct a *search* for parent/family involvement information

http://pfie.ed.gov/faq.php3     U.S. Department of Education 1998 Partnership for Family Involvement in Education facts and link to other sites and publications.

# *Quick Self Check*

## MULTIPLE CHOICE

___ 1. The _____ sociohistorical era viewed the child as a miniature adult and a family had a large extended family.
   a.   premodern
   b.   modern
   c.   postmodern
   d.   none of these

___ 2. The term "family" refers to
  a.   a single mother and several children.
  b.   a blended family with two parents.
  c.   a nuclear family with parents and children.
  d.   all of these

___ 3. The role of a family resource person is all the following **except**
  a.   builds respect and trust between, among, and with families and the community.
  b.   primarily instructional.
  c.   support parents efforts to help children learn at home.
  d.   provide for basic needs.

___ 4. The characteristic of a well-functioning family, which connects extended family members, friends and neighbors, and the community is _____.
  a.   communication.
  b.   shared values.
  c.   social support.
  d.   cohesiveness.

___ 5. Parent involvement efforts over the past several decades have been criticized for being _____.
  a.   inflexible.
  b.   gender-biased.
  c.   non-responsive to family needs.
  d.   all of these

___ 6. Improved home-school relationships are characterized by all the following except _____.
  a.   support.
  b.   communication.
  c.   teacher-friendly policies.
  d.   collaboration.

___ 7. The early childhood practitioner can serve as an advocate for families by
  a.   referring the family to appropriate agencies to meet their needs.
  b.   speaking out to get needed services in the neighborhood.
  c.   both of these
  d.   none of these

___ 8. _____ is an inappropriate family-school interaction practice.
  a.   Frequent face-to-face contacts
  b.   Use of educational jargon

c.   Respond quickly to family's distress signals
   d.   Offering comments, ideas, or suggestions encouraging family's
        exploration

___ 9. By promoting positive family and community relationships, the early childhood
       practitioner gains
   a.   insights into families' concerns and aspirations.
   b.   reinforcement of goals and objectives through home activities.
   c.   successful, self-assured and competent students.
   d.   support from families.
   e.   all of these

___10. _____ is a barrier to effective home-school collaboration.
   a.   Cultural differences
   b.   Time and transportation
   c.   Seeming lack of interest in participating
   d.   all of these


## TRUE/FALSE

___ 1. Understanding families as a social system has little importance.

___ 2. Children and parents influence each other as they adapt over the years.

___ 3. Previous efforts to educate parents were based on three erroneous assumptions:
       (a) learning flows from school to the parent to the child; (b) learning only occurs in
       formal, school-like contexts; and (c) learning should reflect white, middle class
       values.

___ 4. The boundaries separating the responsibilities for children between school and
       home are very clear and distinct.

___ 5. For healthy home-school relationships and the good of each child, the early
       childhood practitioner must confront his/her biases about families.

___ 6. In working with families the early childhood years are no different than any other
       phase of children's education.

___ 7. Collaboration with other professionals is often necessary to find appropriate
       options for helping young children.

___ 8. Positive home-school relationships are not characteristic of effective schools according to research.

___ 9. A partnership model emphasizes the contributions that both parents and practitioners make to promote children's success in school and society.

___10. Understanding the problems or weaknesses of families is an important part of your role in preparing a "family friendly" program.


## SHORT ANSWER

a.      The formal parent/teacher conference is a traditional method of communication between the teacher and family. Describe how you would prepare for and implement a conference listing some specific strategies you would use to begin and end the conference and ways you would try to involve the parent in the discussion.

b.      Why is the effective parent-teacher partnership a critical component of successful early childhood programs?

c.      What are the benefits for families from building a partnership with teachers?

# *Answers*

## Chapter Summary

- growth, development (p. 352)
- (c) roles, (d) adaptability, (f) values (p. 353)
- children's learning (p. 354)

  - ▸ respect
  - ▸ interrelationships
  - ▸ early (p. 354)
- 3. connections, community (p. 355)

- support, collaboration, open communication (p. 357)
  - ▸ parenting, communicating, volunteering, learning at home, decision-making, collaborating   (p. 357)
  - ▸ 2. biases (p. 357);
  - ▸ 4. communication, professionalism
  - ▸ 5. families, communities (p. 359)

- cultural differences, lack of interest, time and transportation, difficult parents, practitioner's lack of knowledge (p.363)
- jargon;

  - – easy
  - – network (p.366)
  - – special concerns
  - – blaming
  - – all (p.367)
  - ▸ specific individuals
  - ▸ agreement (p. 368)
- equal, provide, refer (p. 370)
- empowerment (p. 370)
  - ▸ public policy (p. 371)

  - ▸ public will (p.372)


## Key Terms

*collaboration:* to work jointly with individuals from other agencies or organizations.

*comprehensive service model:*   the provision of all services that a child or family with special needs in one location, often coordinated at the school.

*educare:* refers to the dual activities of education and care performed by early childhood

*empowerment:* helping individuals gain a sense of contro over the events in their lives.

*family:* a post-modern, permeable "social system characterized by a kinship system and by certain sentiments, values, and perceptions" (Elkind, 1995, p. 10).

*family involvement:* commitment of parents to their child's program through a variety of options.

*family resource/support programs:* focus is on the provision of services that will enhance family life.

*parent-teacher conference:* a one-on-one interaction between the teacher and the child's parents or guardians.


## Quick Self Check

### Multiple Choice

| | | | | |
|---|---|---|---|---|
| 1. a | 2. d | 3. b | 4. c | 5. d |
| 6. c | 7. c | 8. b | 9. e | 10. d |


### True/False

1. F    2. T    3. T    4. F    5. T    6. F    7. T    8. F    9. T    10. F


### Short answer

a.    See pages 367 - 369 for suggestions as well as other sections in this chapter and others on communication skills.

b.    See pages 354 - 355, 359,and 361 - 363.

c.    See pages 362 -363.

# Chapter Eleven

## EXPLORING YOUR ROLE AS A PROFESSIONAL IN THE FIELD OF EARLY CHILDHOOD EDUCATION

---

# *Chapter Review...*

## Chapter Learning Outcomes

- Define professional development.
- Reflect upon the stages in teachers' professional growth.
- Develop strategies for managing personal/professional growth.
- Understand the value of a research base to support teaching practice.
- Document growth as an educator through a professional portfolio.

## Chapter Summary

- A professional teacher strives for _____ and is committed to continue learning.

- Four dimensions differentiate a professional role from other types of occupations:
  1) a defined body of specialized _____,
  2) control over licensure,
  3) _____ of practitioners, and
  4) _____ prestige and economic standing.

- A career dedicated to the care and education of children is unique among professions in the following ways:
  - No say about who their "clients" will be
  - The test of a teacher's professional abilities is _____oriented and _____ specific.
  - Although seeming to be focused on adults, teacher education is intended for _____.
  - Reciprocal _____ ties between the professional and client are encouraged in teaching.
  - _____ is the only profession most in the U.S. have observed.

- Teachers identify their needs for professional growth and monitor their own progress toward the goal of becoming better teachers.  The three questions that guide professional development are:
  1.
  2.
  3.

---

***PAUSE AND REFLECT ABOUT***     *YOUR OWN DEVELOPMENT AS A PROFESSIONAL*

1.     **What have you learned?** How would you explain the difference between teaching young children and teaching children at other developmental levels to someone who is unfamiliar with the field of early childhood?

2.     **What will you do?** How do you plan to go about fulfilling the traditional mission of the early childhood educator: educating the whole-child and fostering total learning—cognitive, physical, social and emotional? If you were asked to draw a path or diagram of your hoped-for career, what would it look like?

3.     **Where will you find guidance?** What philosophical or theoretical orientations, powerful ideas, and effective strategies do you use to guide your professional practice?

    Who are your mentors and role models?

    What are your future goals?

- Early childhood care and education are a paradox in that so much is demanded for relatively _____ financial compensation, and such great _____ investment; but that investment is in our nation's greatest resource:_____ .

- Teachers who are maturing as professionals:
  - pursue information about what will help them to teach better
  - Learn from _____ upon their experiences
  - work hard to fulfill the professional _____ they have chosen, and
  - move from _____ on others to greater _____ - _____ and self-_____(Knowles,1975).

- Variables that affect teachers' overall job satisfaction and contribute to their professional development are: _____, programs and systems, _____, democracy, _____, innovation and improvement, and relationships with families and communities.

- Four stages have been identified in the professional development of teachers and are listed below with each's theme:

  Stage 1: Novice                        Theme:_____

  Stage 2: Advanced Beginner             Theme:_____

  Stage 3: _____              Theme: Renewal

  Stage 4: _____              Theme: _____

---

***PAUSE AND REFLECT ABOUT***     *WHAT YOUR METAPHOR IS*

An early childhood administrator had this to say about her role: "I see myself as a change agent, a coach, a mentor, and a facilitator whose job it is to remove obstacles so that people can teach." On her lapel was a button that read "Children First." Early childhood educators use a variety of metaphors or symbols to characterize our professional roles. One teacher from a neighborhood with a high crime rate referred to his classroom as "a safe sector of the city, a haven." And there are other examples on page 395-96 of your text. What metaphors or mottos do you live by as a teacher of the very young? Give this some thought then write them here.

- Becoming an outstanding early childhood teacher depends on the personal investment one makes in one's learning and teaching, keeping _____ at the center of one's practice.

- Teacher preparation programs cannot fully prepare teachers for what they will encounter in the classroom for several reasons:
  - change versus the status quo
  - general preparation versus situation specific
  - real versus _____
  - promise versus _____

- Although beginning teachers share many common concerns, they can address their own personal and professional needs to learn through the following strategies:
  - Observing
  - _____
  - Writing
  - Raising questions
  - Collaborating
  - Using _____

# Activities...

**Key Terms**   Match Column A with Column B.

| | Column A | | Column B |
|---|---|---|---|
| ___1. | documents produced in the normal course of work of the individual developing a portfolio | a. | procedural knowledge |
| ___2. | professional knowledge acquired through direct experience | b. | episodic knowledge |
| ___3. | professional knowledge gained from personally meaningful, deeply affecting events | c. | preservice teacher |
| ___4. | an image or phrase that symbolizes something else and captures the essence of something profound | d. | professional portfolio |
| ___5. | an individual in the process of making a career decision about teaching | e. | professional development |
| ___6. | professional knowledge of the physical sequence of events associated with a task | f. | artifacts |

____ 7. the systematic and ongoing process toward the goal of improvement as a teacher; or "providing occasions for teachers to reflect critically on their practice and to fashion new knowledge and beliefs about content, pedagogy, and learners" (Darling-Hammond & McLaughlin, 1995, p.597)

____ 8. a selected collection of one's professional work which documents success in teaching

____ 9. an intrinsic code of ethics, values, commitments, and responsibilities that guide thoughts and actions

____10. terms, facts, concepts and principles learned through reading

g.  case knowledge

h.  propositional knowledge

i.  professionalism

j.  metaphor

## Project Suggestion

With another student or two, investigate early childhood programs in your local community to learn the types of settings and sponsorship. See chapter 1 for a starting list. Request salary information from school districts, nursery schools, child care centers, family child care homes etc. within your region of the country. Chart and discuss your findings .

## Application Activities

❖  *Meet the Teachers*    After reading about the professional activities of Ms. Huong, Ms. Wilden, and Ms. Renzulli in this feature on pages 383-4, respond to these questions.

   *Compare:*    *What are some of the commonalities among these three teachers, even though they work in different settings and are at different stages in their careers?*

   *Contrast:*    *How do these teachers think about teaching? About learning? How would you characterize the outlook of each one?*

*Connect:* *Reflective teachers are* <u>open minded</u>, *willing to admit or consider that they are wrong;* <u>responsible</u>, *willing to look at the consequences of their actions; and* <u>wholehearted</u>, *willing to accept all students and to practice what they preach (Grant & Zeicher, 1984). What evidence did you see of these characteristics in the three teachers profiled? How will you go about becoming more wholehearted, responsible, and open-minded in your teaching?*

❖ *Ask the Expert:* Sharon Lynn Kagan talks about two common misconceptions that students and novice advocates often voice in reference to public policy creation and leadership. Read this section on pages 402-403.

◆ What are the two misconceptions?

◆ What are the roles of leader and policy advocate in early care and education?

◆ What do you know about these roles?

◆ What do you need to find out?

❖ *Featuring Families*: One of the characteristics of a professional early childhood practitioner is the ability to interact with parents and families to build mutual trust and respect. This feature on pages 389-390 provides a sample of the information gathered during a home visit with the family of second grader, Jesus Martinez.

♦ Develop lists of pros and cons for conducting home visits.

♦ What information can only be gained through a home visit?

## Chapter 11 Observation

Attend a *local meeting* of one of the following professional organizations: National Association for the Education of Young Children (NAEYC), Association for Childhood Education International (ACEI), Southern Early Childhood Association(SECA), the National Education Association (NEA). Before you go to the meeting find out about the organization, its publications, and the cost for membership. The group may have a national web page with this information. Review the promotional materials about the organization. Then...

♦ Report on your impressions of the organization after the meeting and a review of their materials. Would this organization be helpful to you as a teacher?

♦ If so, in what ways?

♦ If not, why would you **not** consider membership.

## *Journal Entry*

After reading the *One Child, Three Perspectives* on pages 403-404, respond to the following *React/Research/Reflect* questions.

♦ **React** In what ways are the perspectives of the three adults alike? Which perspective do you identify most strongly with, and why?

♦ **Research** Locate information on spina bifida at the library. What are some of the ways of helping children with this condition to be accepted by their peers and have successful learning experiences?

♦ **Reflect** Rolando's mother, father, and the Head Start teacher have definite ideas about how to meet this young child's needs. What might be the underlying reasons for these differences? How do they compare with what you have read?

## Authentic Assessment

Develop a personal professional development plan. First, respond in writing to the first "Timeless Question" - Who am I? What skills, knowledge, and dispositions do I bring to my role as a preservice teacher? Then using the Performance Standards for Beginning Teachers and the Components for Professional Practice, outline what you need to be an effective teacher of young children. Finally, select 3 to 5 of your 'needs' and develop a plan to meet your needs. Create a grid in which you list your needs across the top and the Strategies for Professional Development along the left side margin. Explore course offerings, books, workshops, professional organizations, the Internet and other potential activities within your school and community to fill in your grid, including the name of activity and pertinent information (such as date, location, speaker, title). Leave a space in each square to indicate the completion of the activity listed and some blank squares to add additional activities.

Professional Development Needs:

4.

5.

6.

7.

8.

| Strategies / Professional Development Needs | Need # 1: | Need # 2: | Need #3: |
|---|---|---|---|
| 1. | | | |
| 2. | | | |
| 3. | | | |
| 4. | | | |
| | | | |
| | | | |

# Resources...

## Videos and other audio-visual materials...

*Careers in Child Development* (11 min.) (1990). Insight Media.

*Career Encounters: Early Childhood Education* (28 min.). NAEYC.

*Celebrating Early Childhood Teachers* (22 min.). NAEYC.

*Seeds of Change-Leadership and Staff Development* (30 min.) Part 8 - The Early Childhood Program: A Place to Learn and Grow. NAEYC.

### Additional Reading...

Baptiste, N. & Sheerer, M. (1997). Negotiating the challenges of the "survival" stage of professional development. *Early Childhood Education Journal, 24*(4), 265-268.

Bredekamp, S. & Willer, B. (1993). Professionalizing the field of early childhood education: Pros and Cons. *Young Children, 48*, 82-84.

Dresden, J. & Myers, B. (1989). Early childhood professionals: Toward self-definition. *Young Children, 44*(2), 62-66.

Jalongo, M. R. & Isenberg, J. P. (1995). *Teachers' stories: From personal narrative to professional insight.* San Francisco, CA: Jossey-Bass.

Johnson, J. & McCracken, J. (Eds.) (1994). *The Early Childhood Career Lattice: Perspectives on Professional Development.* Washington, DC: NAEYC.

Katz, L. (1995). *Talks with Teachers of Young Children.* Norwood, NJ: Ablex.

Kontos, S. (1991). Family day care: Out of the shadows and into the limelight. Washington, DC: NAEYC.

Paley, V. G. (1997). *The Girl with the Brown Crayon.* Cambridge, MA: Cambridge University Press.

Walling, D. (Ed.) (1994). *Teachers as Leaders.* Bloomington, IN: Phi Delta Kappa Educational Foundation.

# *Quick Self Check*

## MULTIPLE CHOICE

___ 1. Professionalism guides the thoughts and actions by referring to
    a.    intrinsic code of ethics.
    b.    values.
    c.    commitments.
    d.    responsibilities.
    e.    all of these

___ 2. Which of the following are dimensions that differentiates a professional role from other occupations?
    a.    specialized body of knowledge
    b.    control over licensure
    c.    having a code of conduct
    d.    autonomy of practice
    e.    a, b, and d

___ 3. Education differs from other professions because
    a.    clients are adults - parents and the community.
    b.    professional abilities are evaluated through paper and pencil testing.
    c.    emotional ties between professional and client are discouraged.
    d.    everyone has had an opportunity to observe.
    e.    all of the above

___ 4. In early childhood care and education, the specialized knowledge which teachers are expected to master includes
    a.    case knowledge.
    b.    logical/mathematical knowledge.
    c.    procedural knowledge.
    d.    pedagogical knowledge.
    e.    a and c
    f.    all of the above

___ 5. Some of the things that shock new teachers in their first teaching position include
    a.    the amount of paperwork.
    b.    the range and intensity of students' needs.
    c.    parents lack of confidence.
    d.    lack of institutional support.

e. all of these

f. none of these

____ 6. The question most identified with the proficient teacher is,

a. Who am I?

b. How can I grow in competence and confidence?

c. Am I cut out to be a teacher?

d. What will I do to improve my experience rather than diminish my effectiveness?

e. What impact has my life had on the lives of children and families?

____ 7. Generally to teach at the community college or associate degree level, an individual needs as a minimum

a. a Child Development Associate (CDA) certificate and experience.

b. a bachelors' degree in early childhood or child development.

c. a master's degree in early childhood or child development and significant experience working with young children.

d. a doctorate in early childhood or child development, prior experience with children and college level teaching experience.

____ 8. The early childhood practitioner must be a life-long learner because

a. teacher preparation programs cannot fully prepare an individual for all they will encounter in the classroom.

b. as a human being, the practitioner is always changing.

c. the policies, requirements, and knowledge base for early childhood care and education are continually changing.

d. all of the above

____ 9. Student teachers and beginning teachers are often worried about which of the following questions?

a. How will I respond to misbehavior?

b. What if my supervising teacher and I don't get along?

c. Will I have enough time to plan effectively for all aspects of the curriculum?

d. How will a future employer evaluate me?

e. a, b, and c

f. all of the above

____ 10. Professional teaching portfolios are important to professional growth because they

a. promote self-analysis and critical reflection.

b.    document learning, growth and development over time.
c.    prepares the teacher to work in schools where more balanced and comprehensive forms of assessment are used.
d.    all of the above

TRUE and FALSE

___ 1.  In the United States, it is generally true that the younger the children the lower the status and salary of the practitioner.

___ 2.  Teachers' professional development moves from self-direction to dependence.

___ 3.  A benefit of classroom research conducted by teachers is that teachers develop a deeper understanding of the learning process.

___ 4.  The best teachers are those who reflect deeply about their personal/professional role as teachers, their knowledge about children, subject matter, and teaching methods, the impact of their teaching on children's learning, and the quality of their interactions with children.

___ 5.  A teacher should include every teaching theme, unit, or web that she has developed in her professional portfolio.

___ 6.  Democracy and environments have no influence on teachers' professional development.

___ 7.  Attendance at statewide or regional early childhood conferences is one way to continue to grow professionally.

___ 8.  NAEYC suggests that early care and education professionals should wait until they are permanent employees to learn about the profession's code of ethical conduct.

___ 9.  Developing as a professional depends on one's commitment to continue to learn, even after one has completed an initial or advanced preparation program.

___10.  Teachers who learn to take care of themselves are selfish.

Short Answer

a.    Why is it important for early childhood practitioners to have specialized training?

b.    Is early childhood education a profession?  Explain your answer.  What makes it
      unique?

# *Answers*

## Chapter Review

- excellence (p. 385)
- 1. knowledge, 3. autonomy, 4. high (p. 385)
- performance,
    - situation (p. 385)
    - children
    - emotional
    - teaching (p. 386)

- 1. Who am I?   2. What do I need?   3. How can I get help?  (p. 388)

- small, emotional, children (p. 389)
- reflecting
    - roles, dependence
    - self-direction, evaluation (p. 390)
- people, roles, environments (p. 391)
- Stage 1: survival (p. 393); Stage 2: consolidation, Stage 3: proficient (p. 394);

Stage 4: expert, maturity (p. 395)

- ► children (p. 396)
- ► ideal (p. 398); perfection (p. 398)
- ► participating (p. 400); resources (p. 401)


## Key Terms

1. f    2. g    3. b    4. j    5. c    6. a    7. e    8. d    9. i    10. h

## *Quick Self Check*

### Multiple Choice

| | | | | |
|---|---|---|---|---|
| 1. a | 2. e | 3. d | 4. e | 5. e |
| 6. b | 7. c | 8. d | 9. e | 10. d |

### True/False

1. T    2. F    3. T    4. T    5. F    6. F    7. T    8. F    9. T    10. F

### Short answer

a. Specialized knowledge is one of the characteristics of a profession. More importantly, research has shown that early childhood teachers need specialized training to meet the needs of their multiple roles. See pages 385 - 389.

b. See pages 385 - 87. Answer should include the four agreed upon dimensions of a profession, as well as the 5 areas, which make early childhood education unique.

# Appendix

## Lesson Plan Forms

- Short planning form

- Long planning form

- Narrative Observation Form

## Lesson/Activity Plan - Short Form

I.     **Activity or Lesson Topic (name):**

II.     **Lesson Overview (Goals, concepts, skills):**

III.     **Teaching Procedures:**

IV.     **Materials:**

V.     **Assessment :**

VI.     **Other comments:**

# Lesson/Activity Plan - Long Form

I.      Activity or Lesson Topic (name):

II.     Time:

III.    Lesson Overview:
    A.      Concept:

    B.      Objectives: Students will...

    C.      Grouping pattern:

IV.     Teaching/Learning Procedures:
    A.      Objectives for each group:

    B.      Introductory Activities:

    C.      Developmental Activities:

    D.      Summary Activity:

    E.      Extensions:

V.      Materials:
    A.      Students:

    B.      Teacher:

VI.     Family-School Connection:

VII.     Adaptations for Individual Learners:




VIII.    Orchestration and Monitoring:




IX.      Assessment:




X.       Lesson Effectiveness:
         A.      Objectives:



         B.      Self/Teaching:

## Narrative Observation Form

Child's Name:_____ Child's Age (yrs.)_____(mo.)_____

Setting (Place/Area/Conditions)_____ Date_____Time_____

Observation # or Focus_____

| Time | Description | Interpretation/Comments |
|------|-------------|-------------------------|
|      |             |                         |